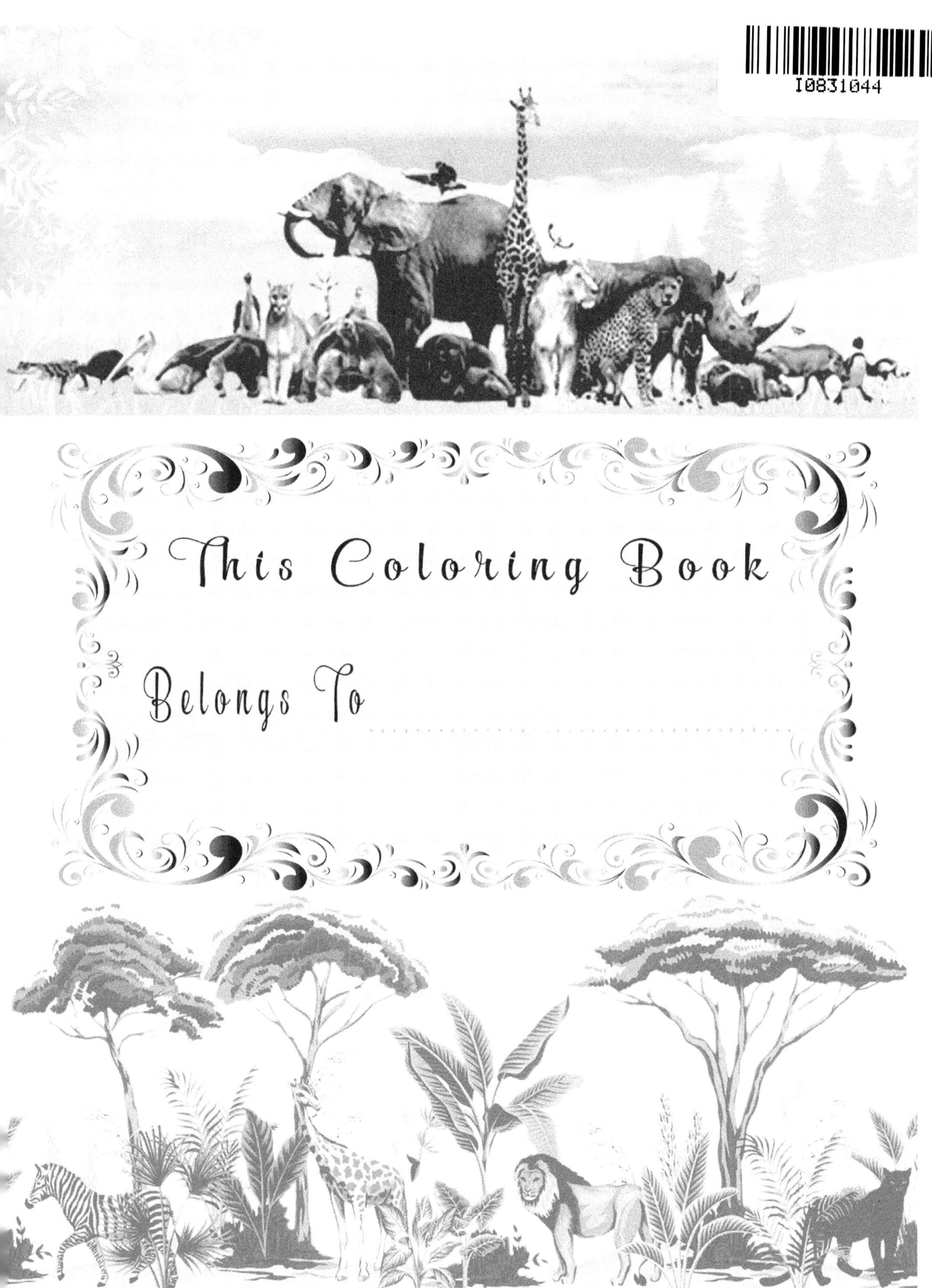

This Coloring Book
Belongs To

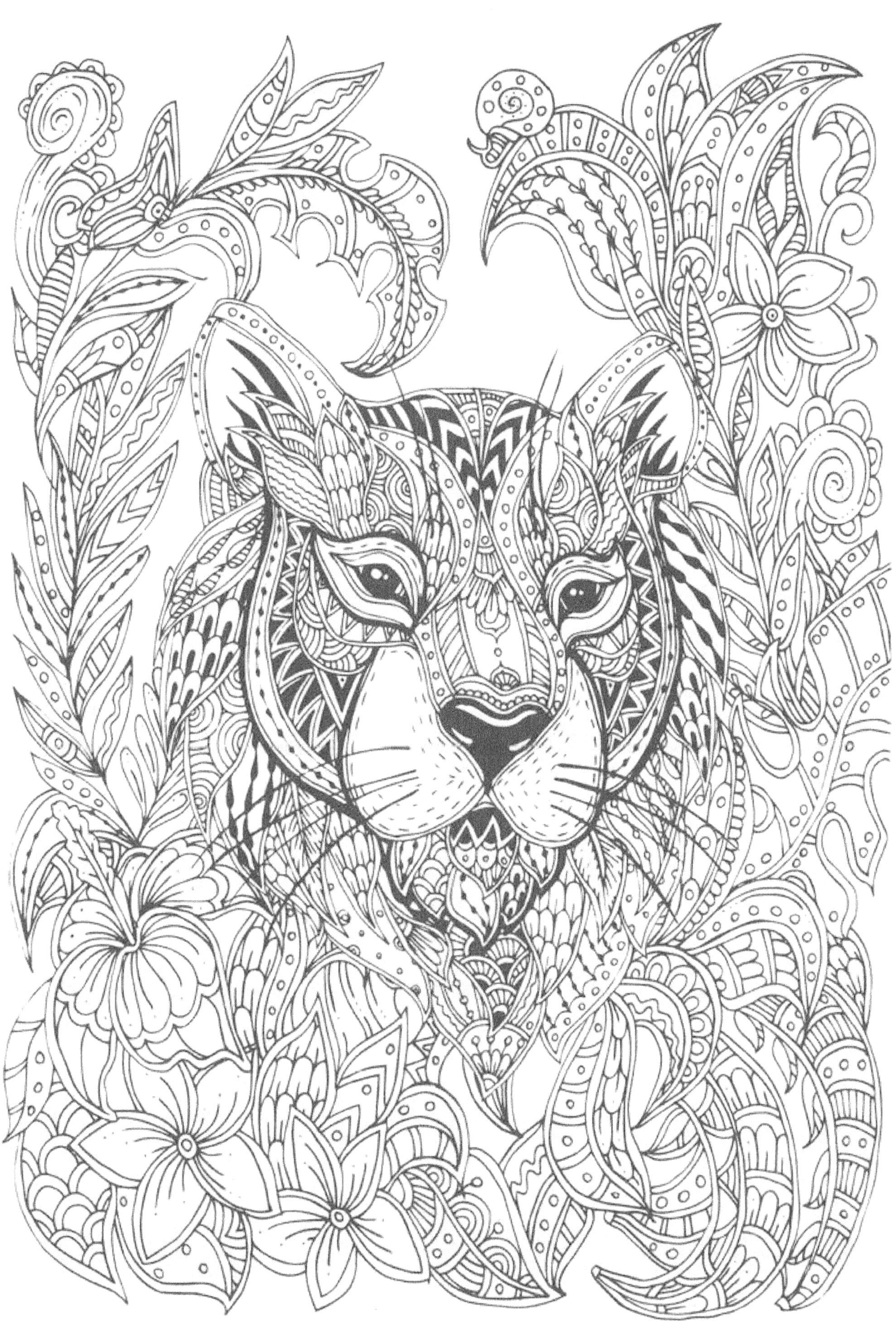

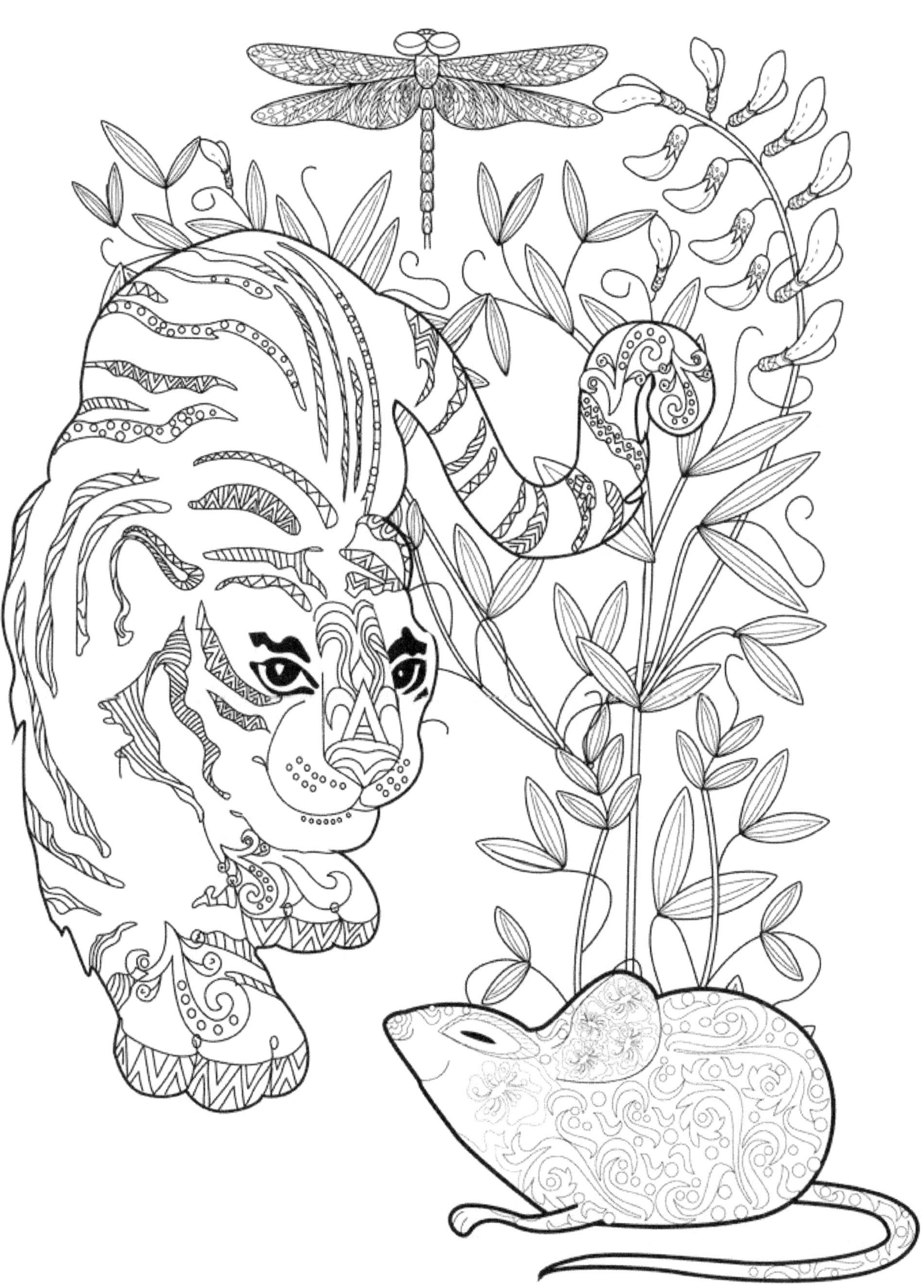

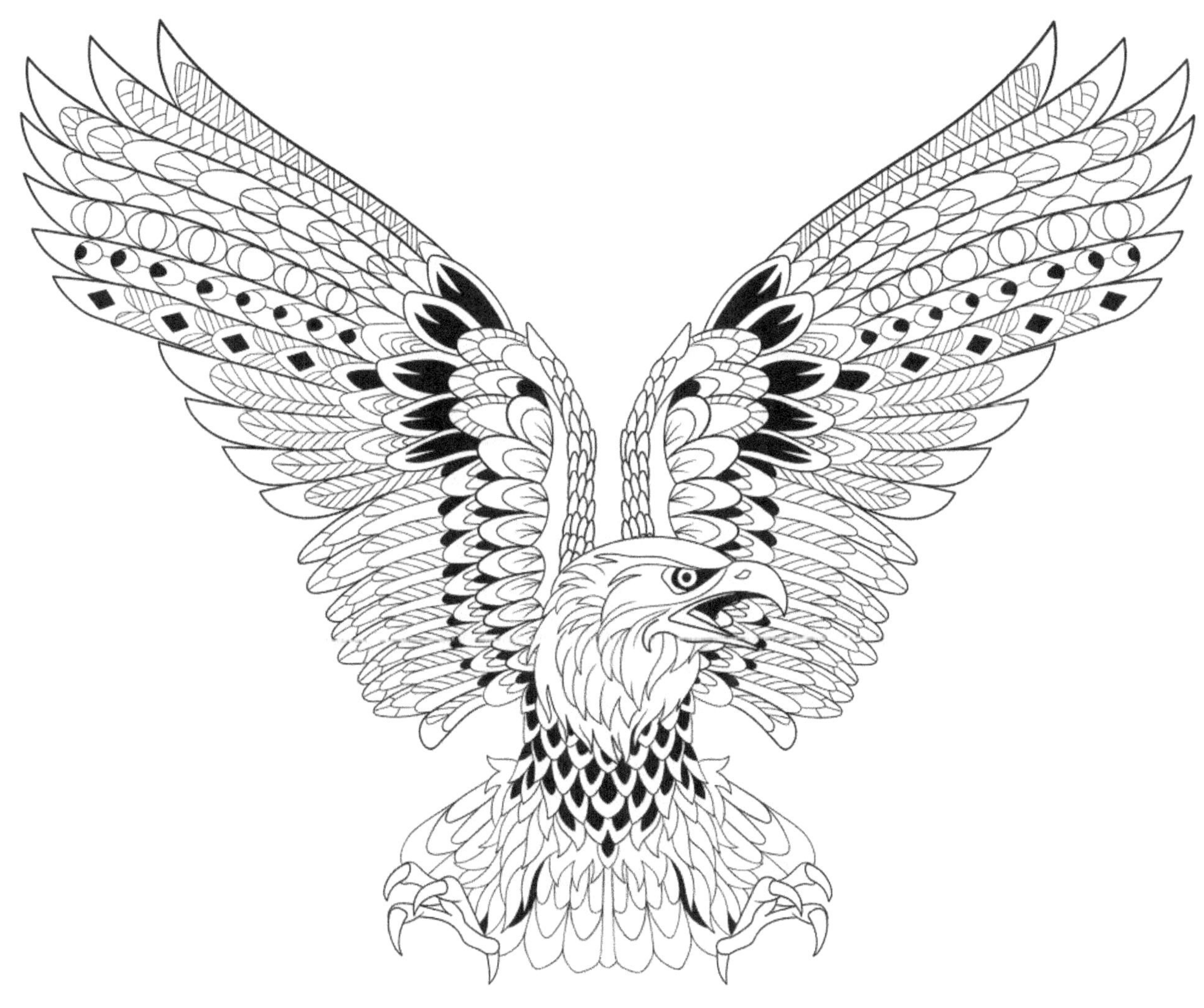

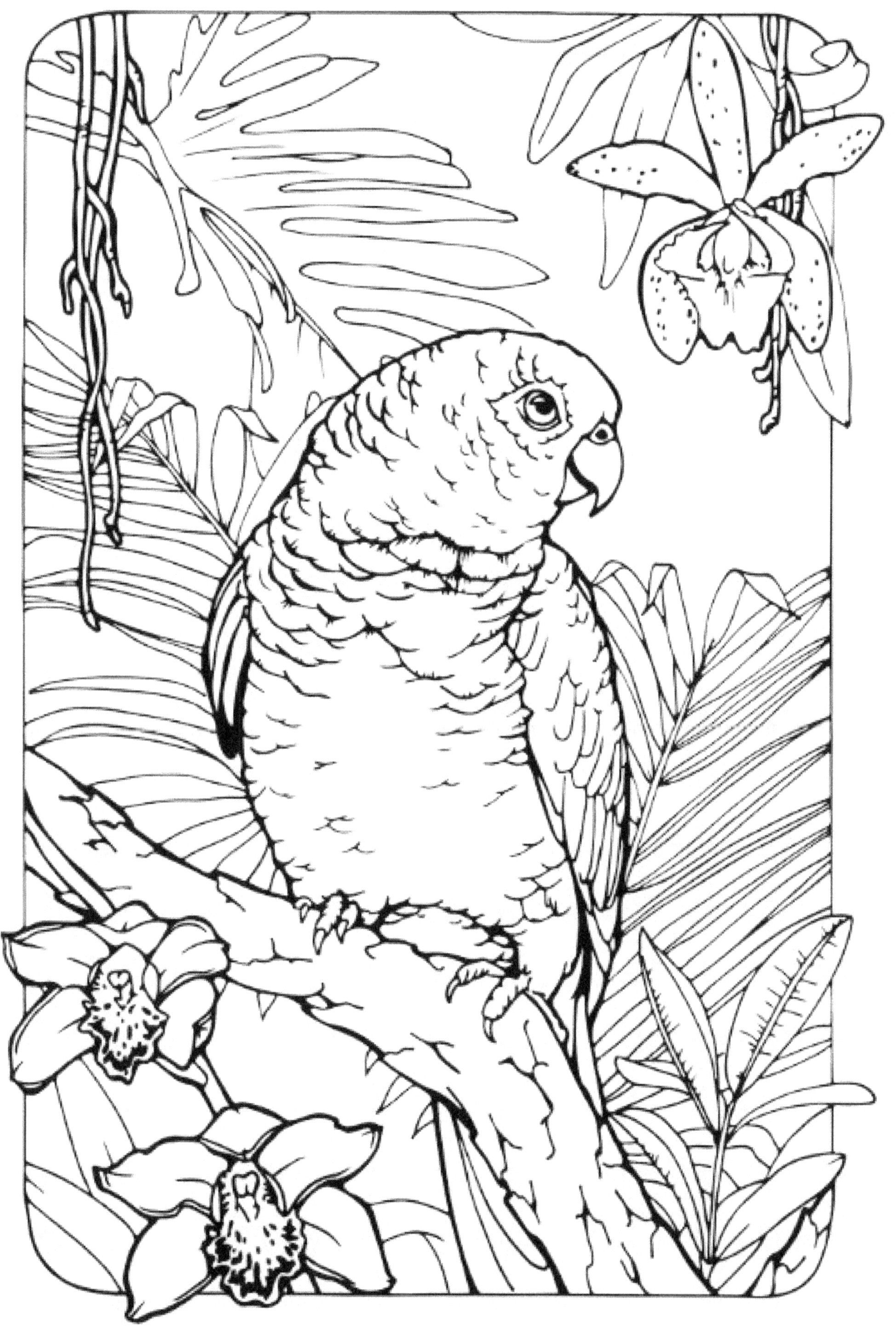

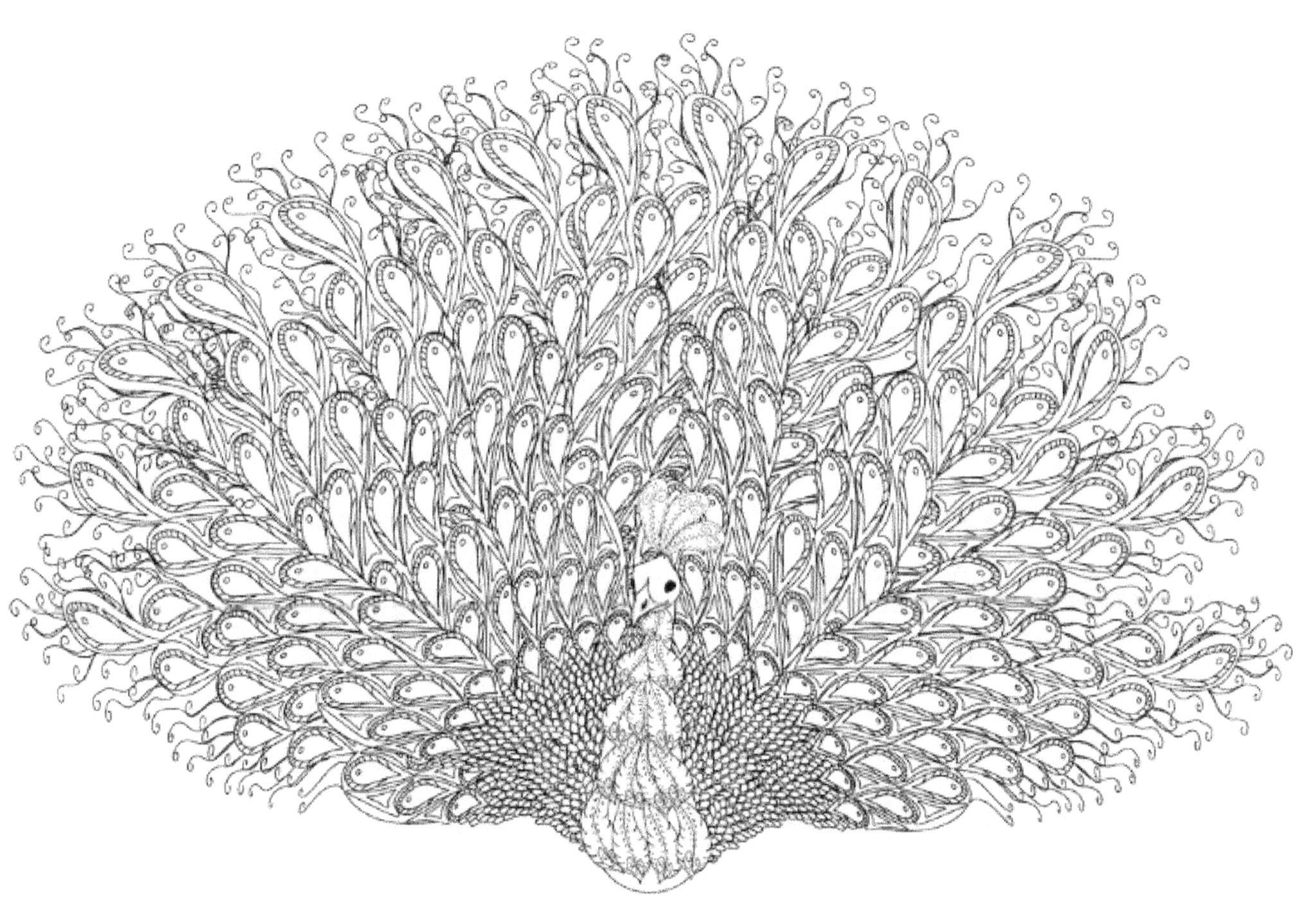

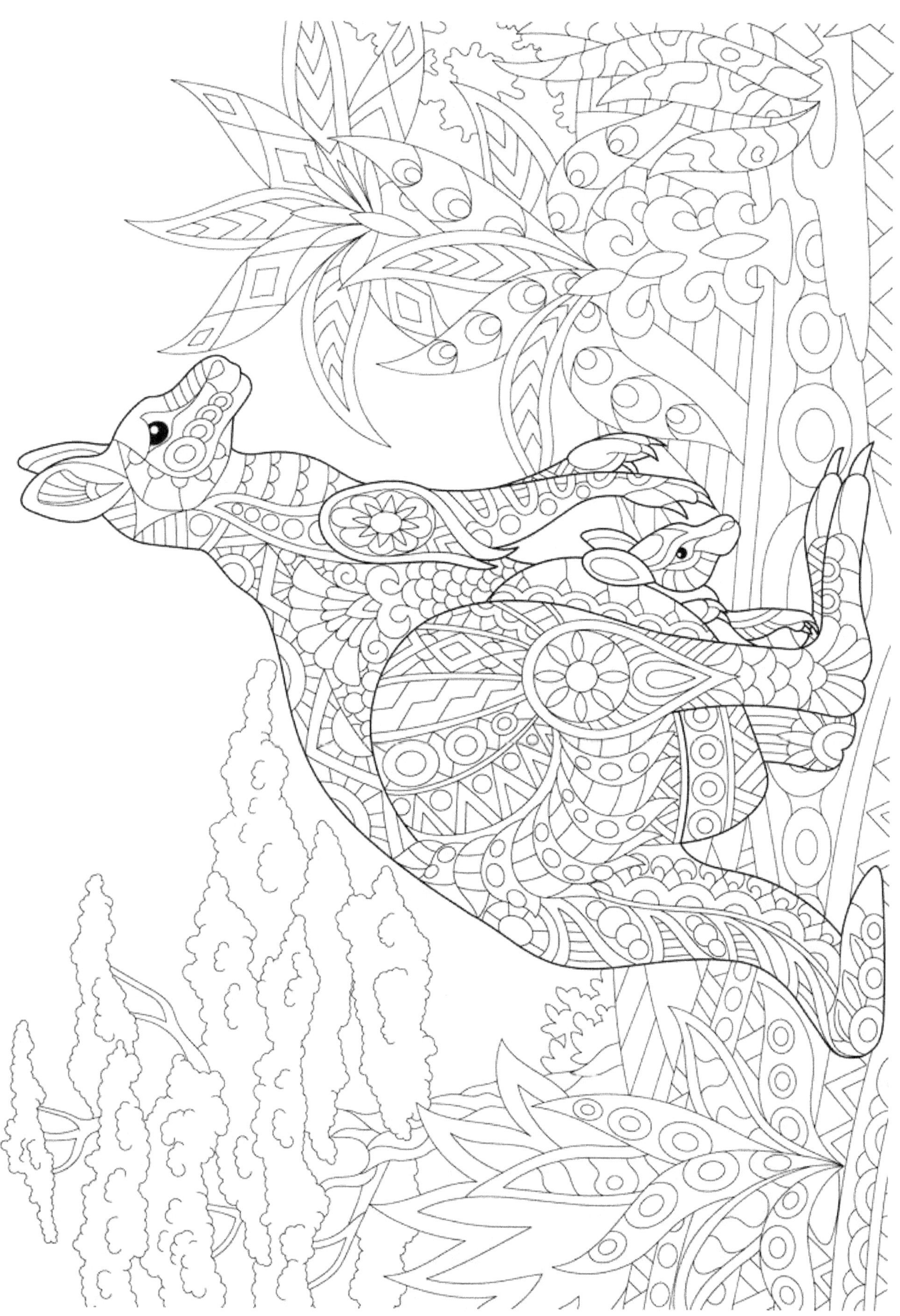

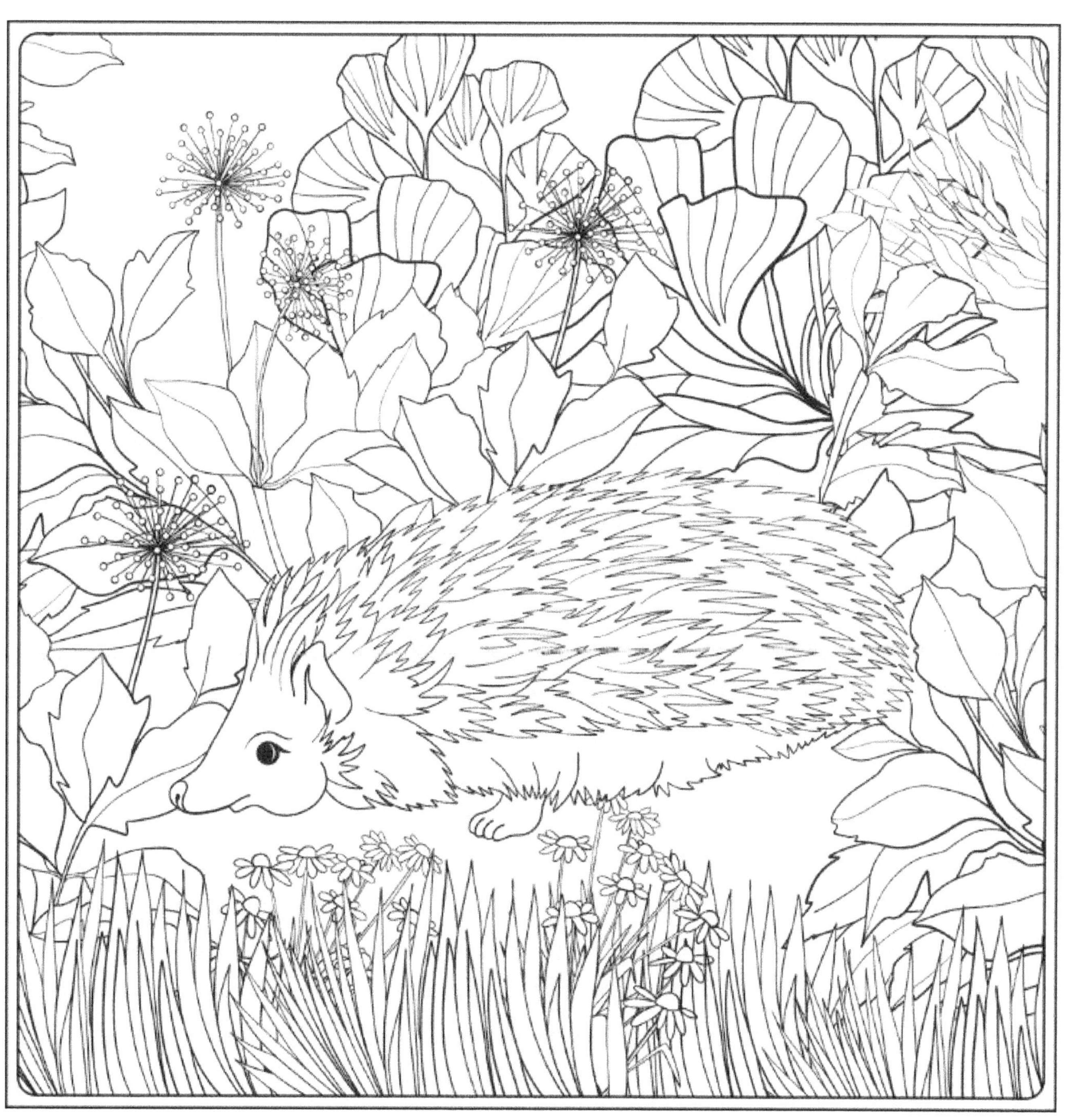

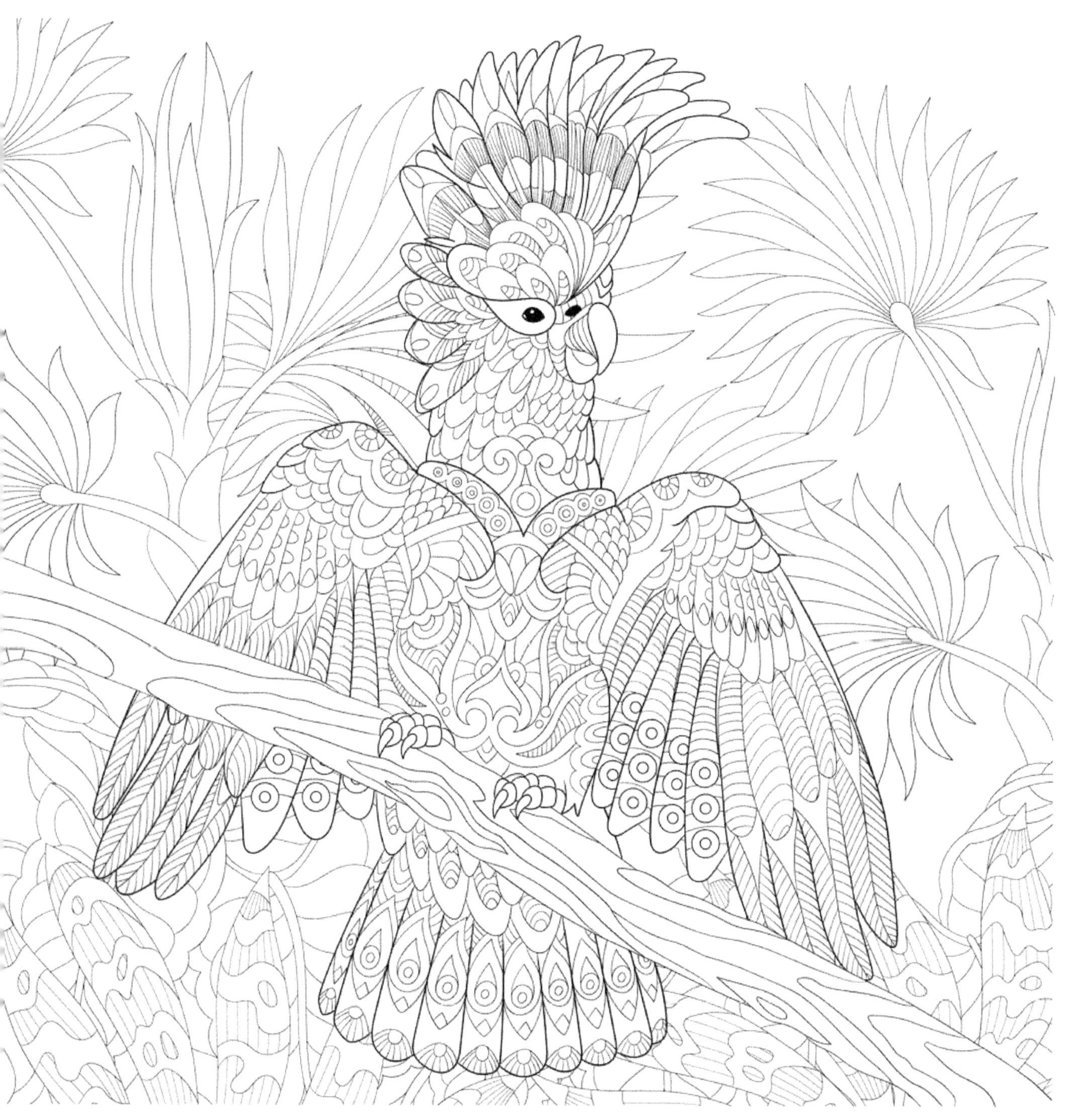

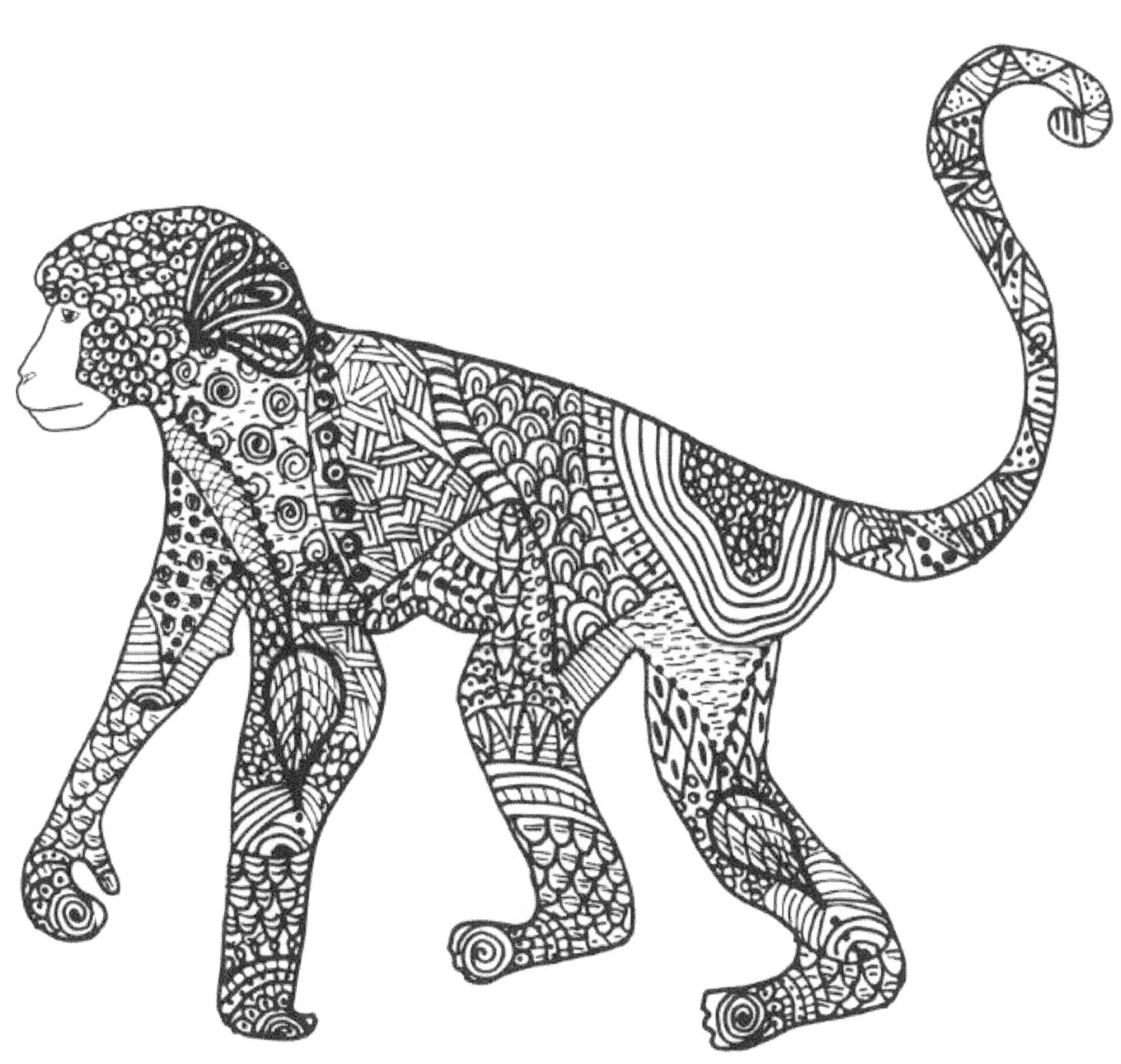

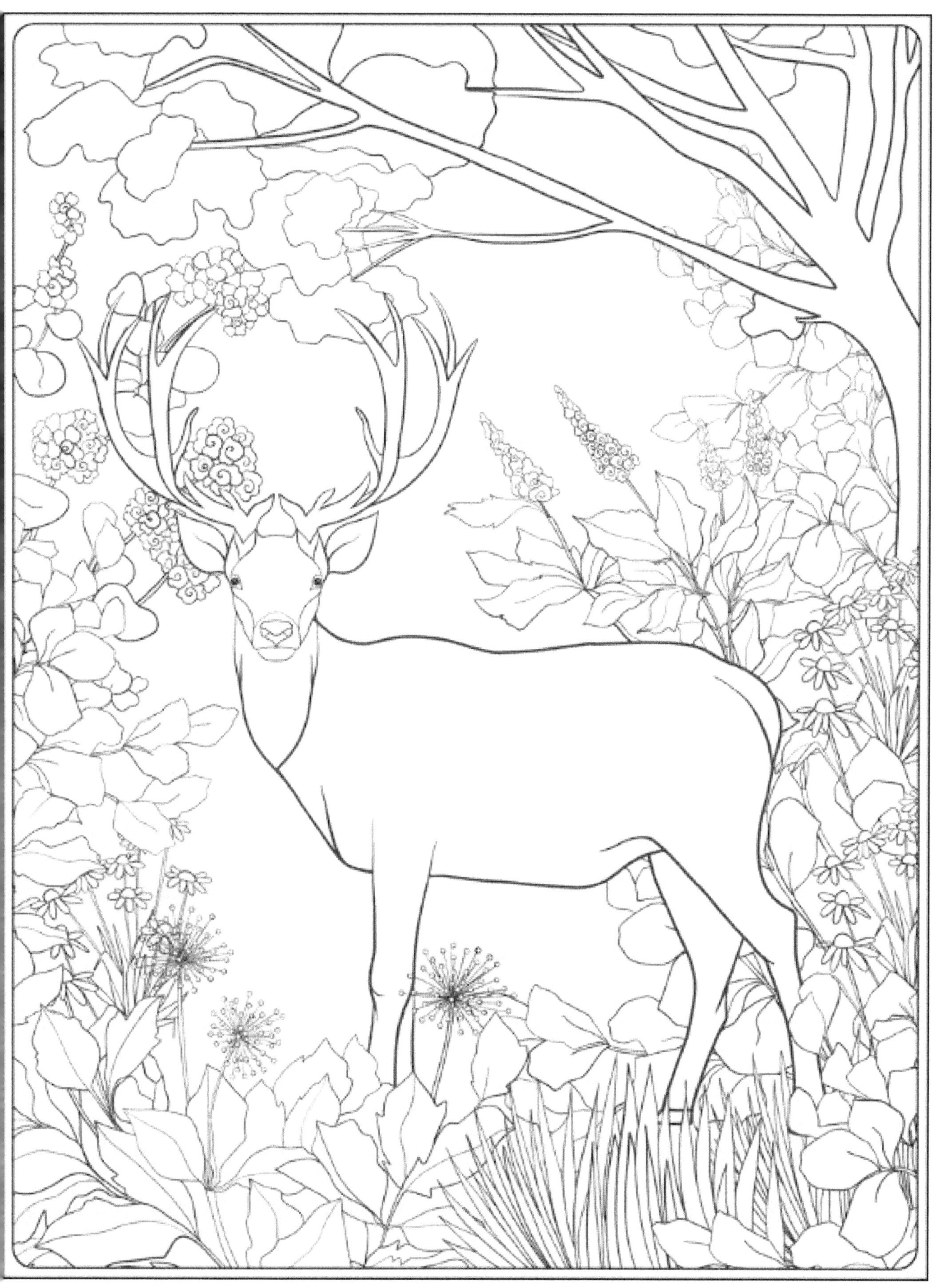

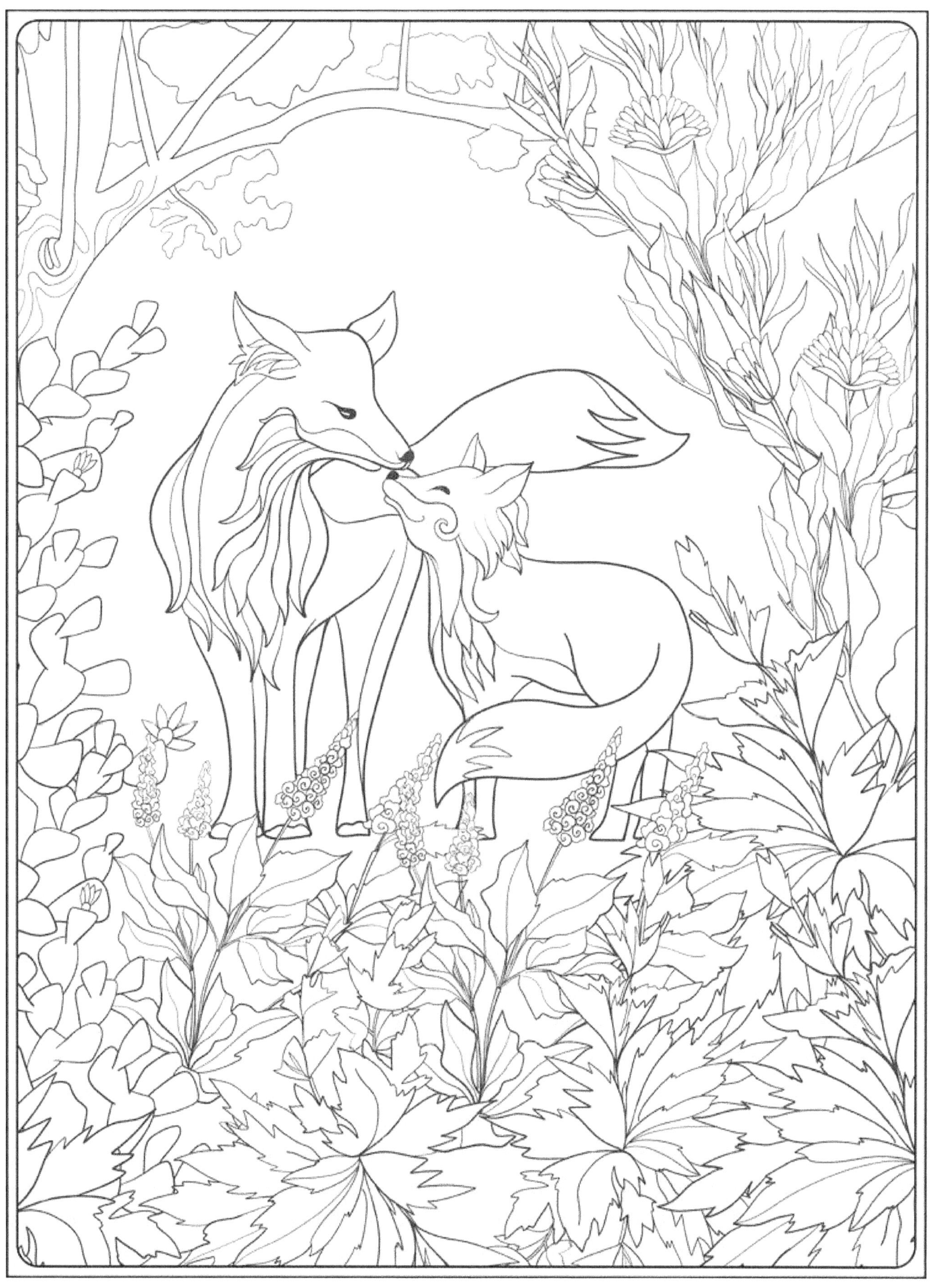

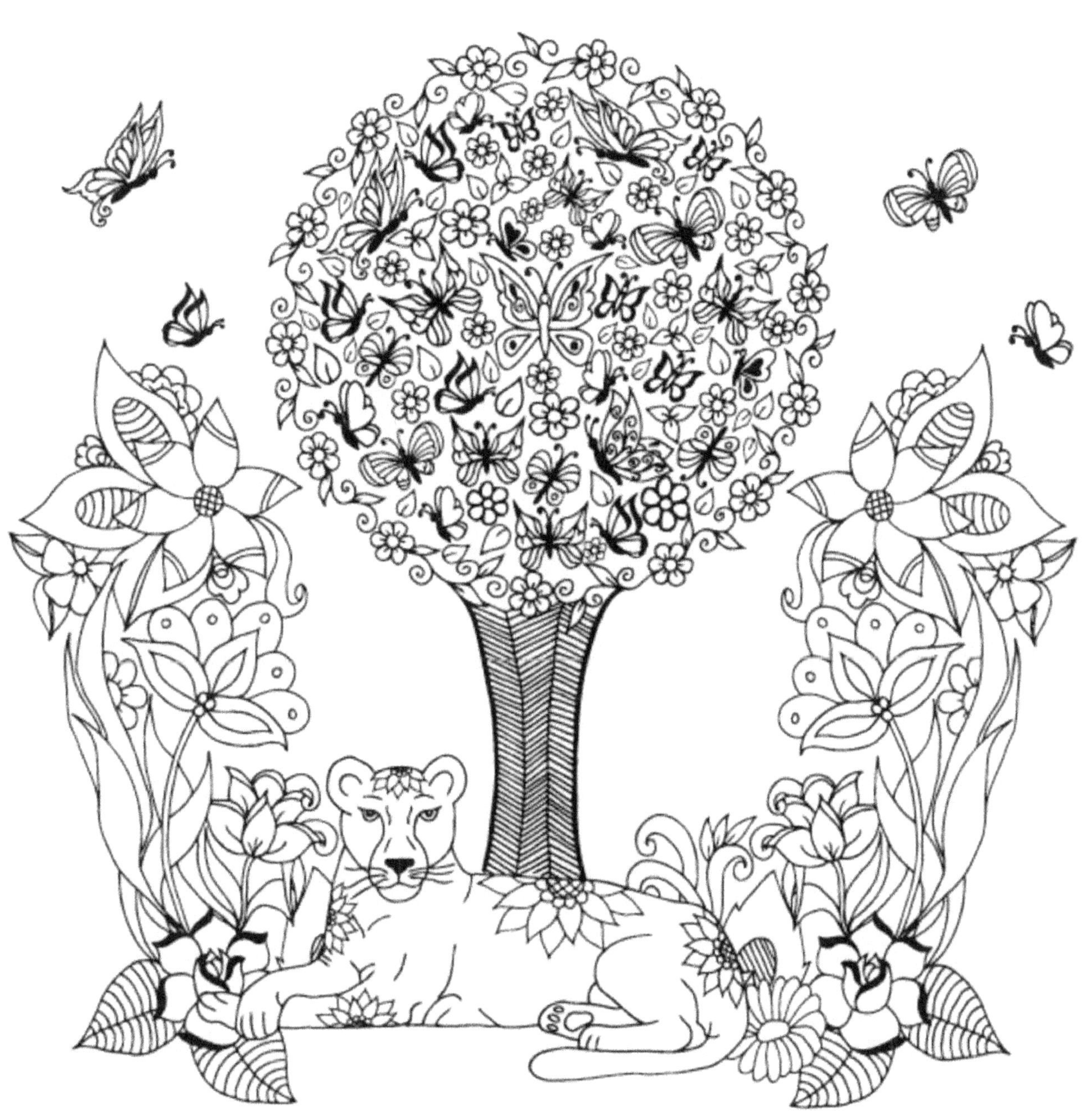

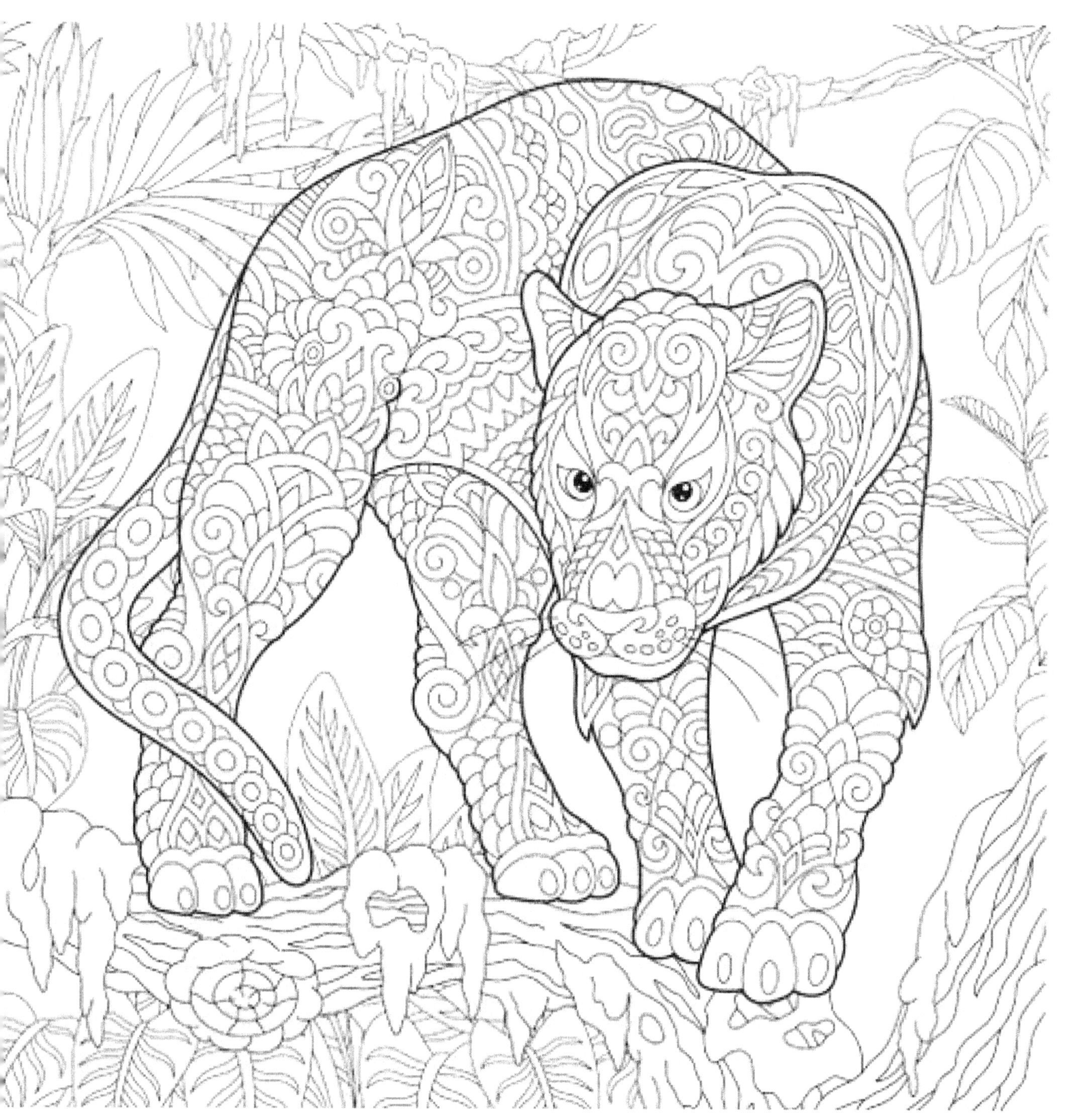

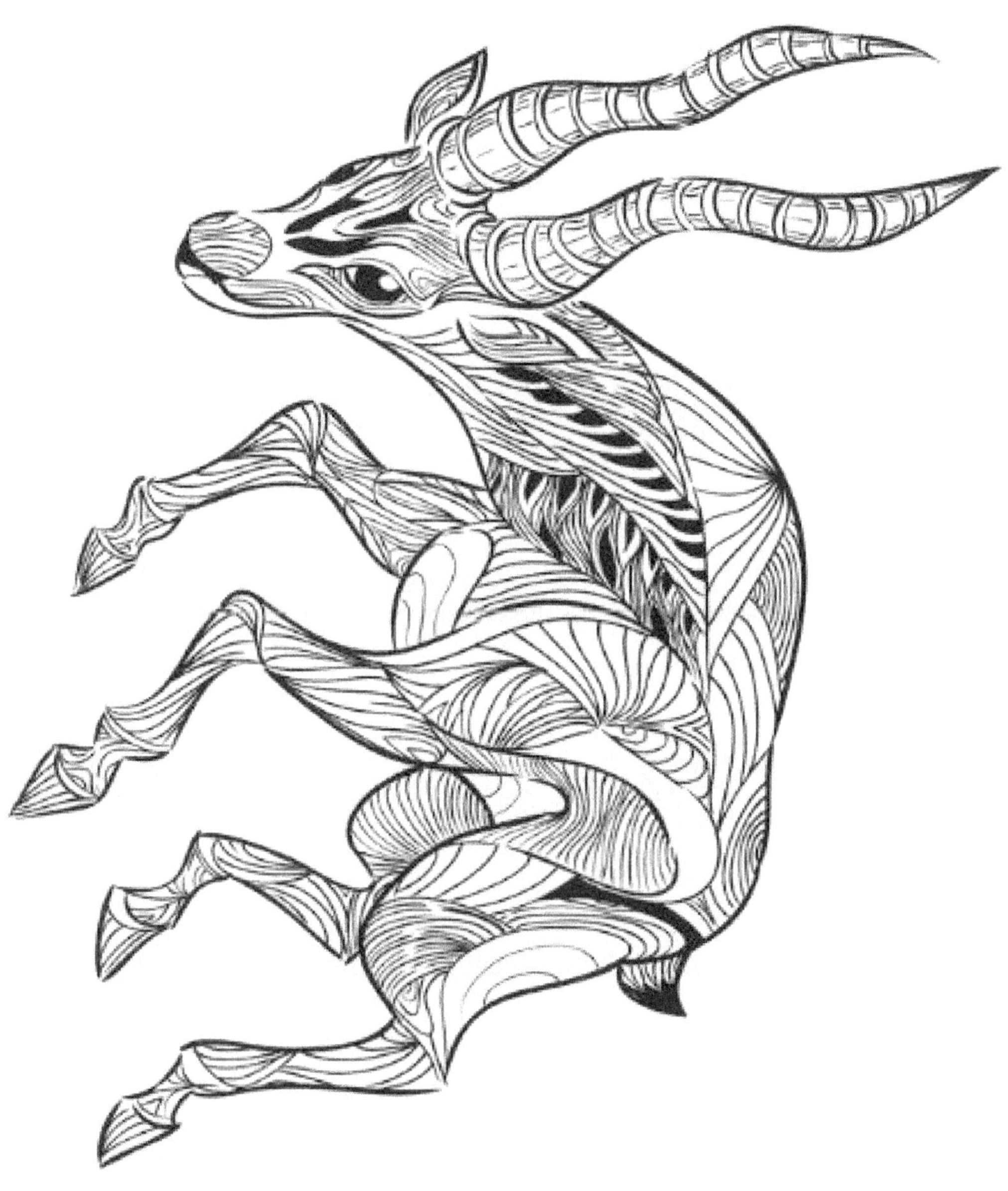

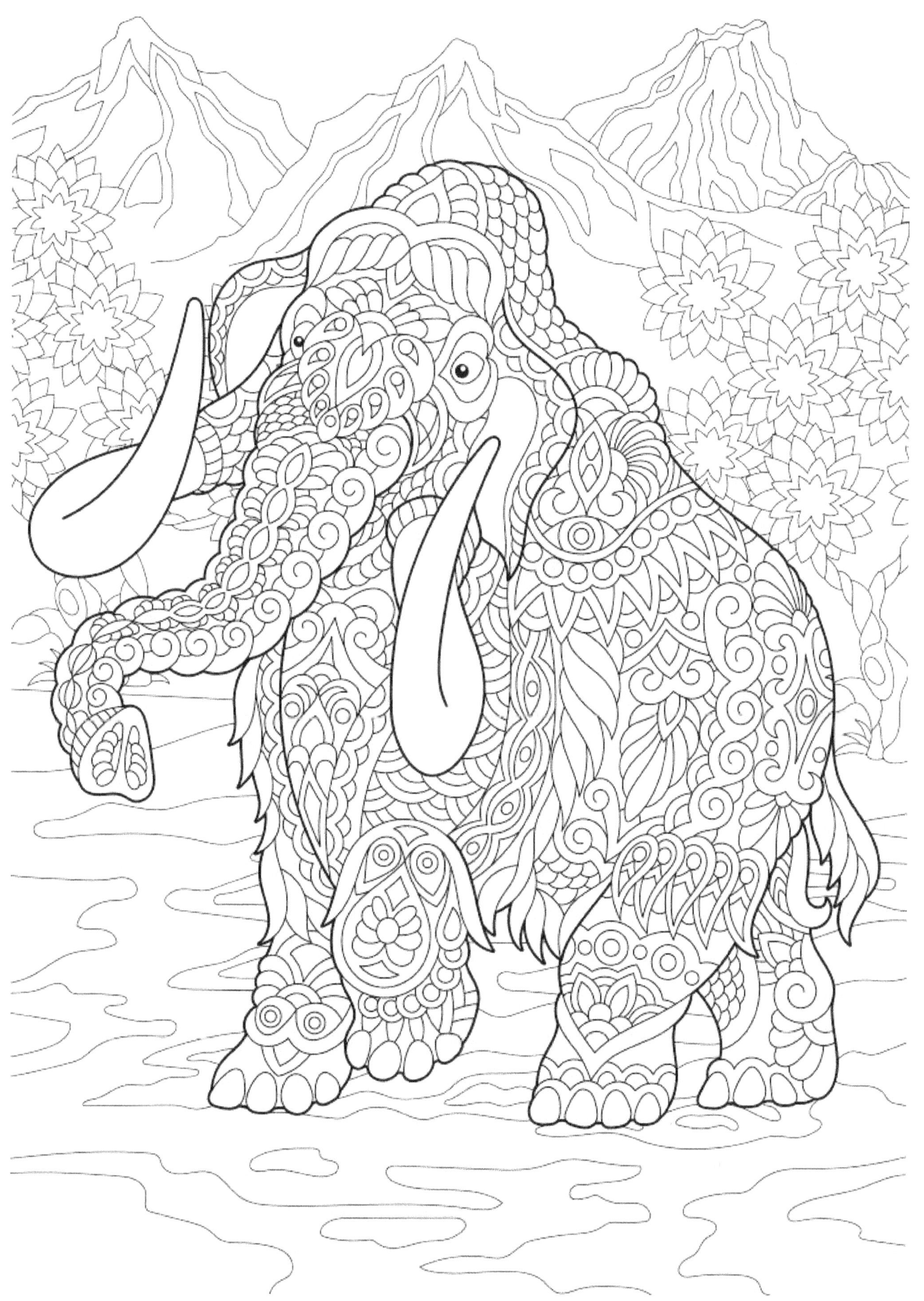

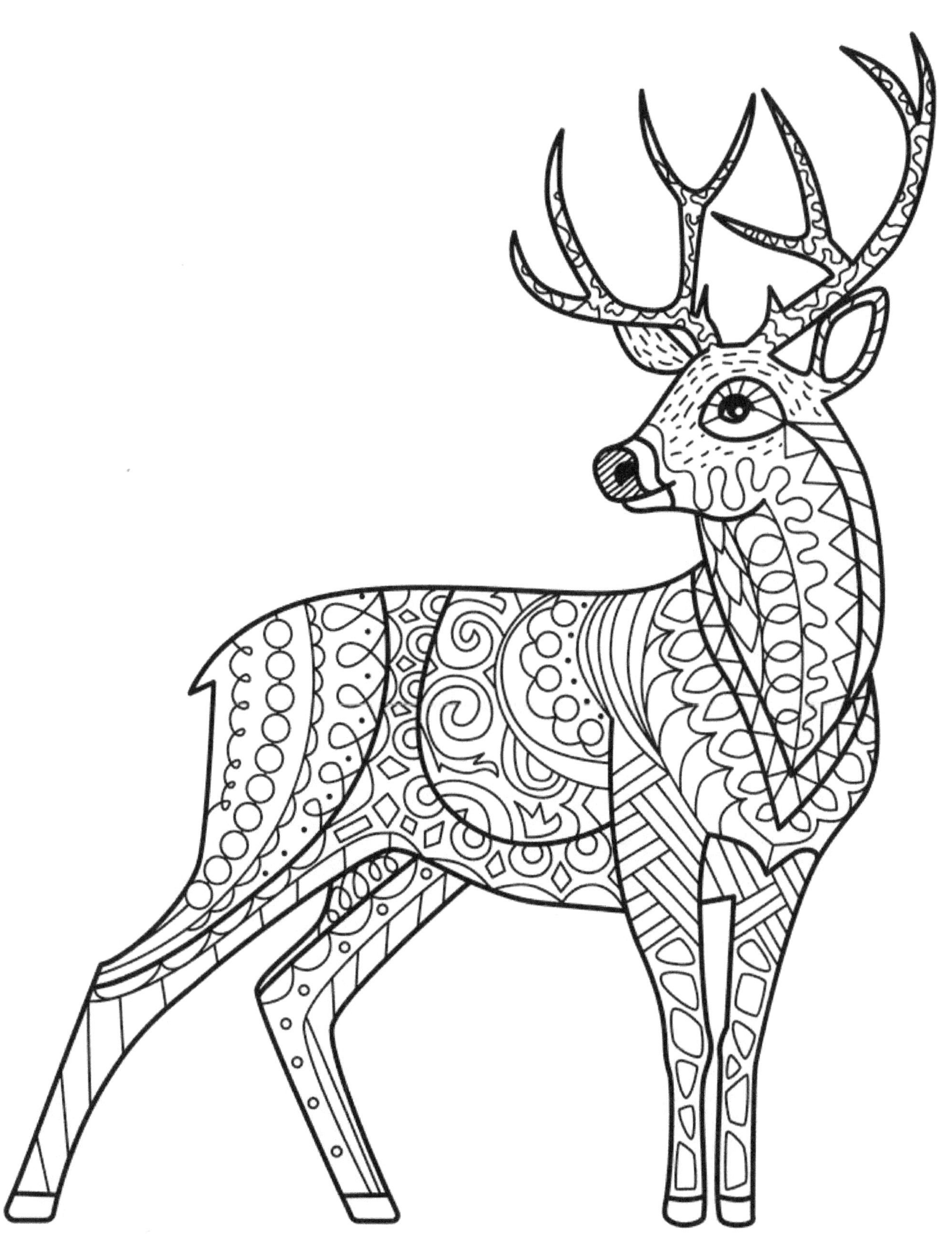

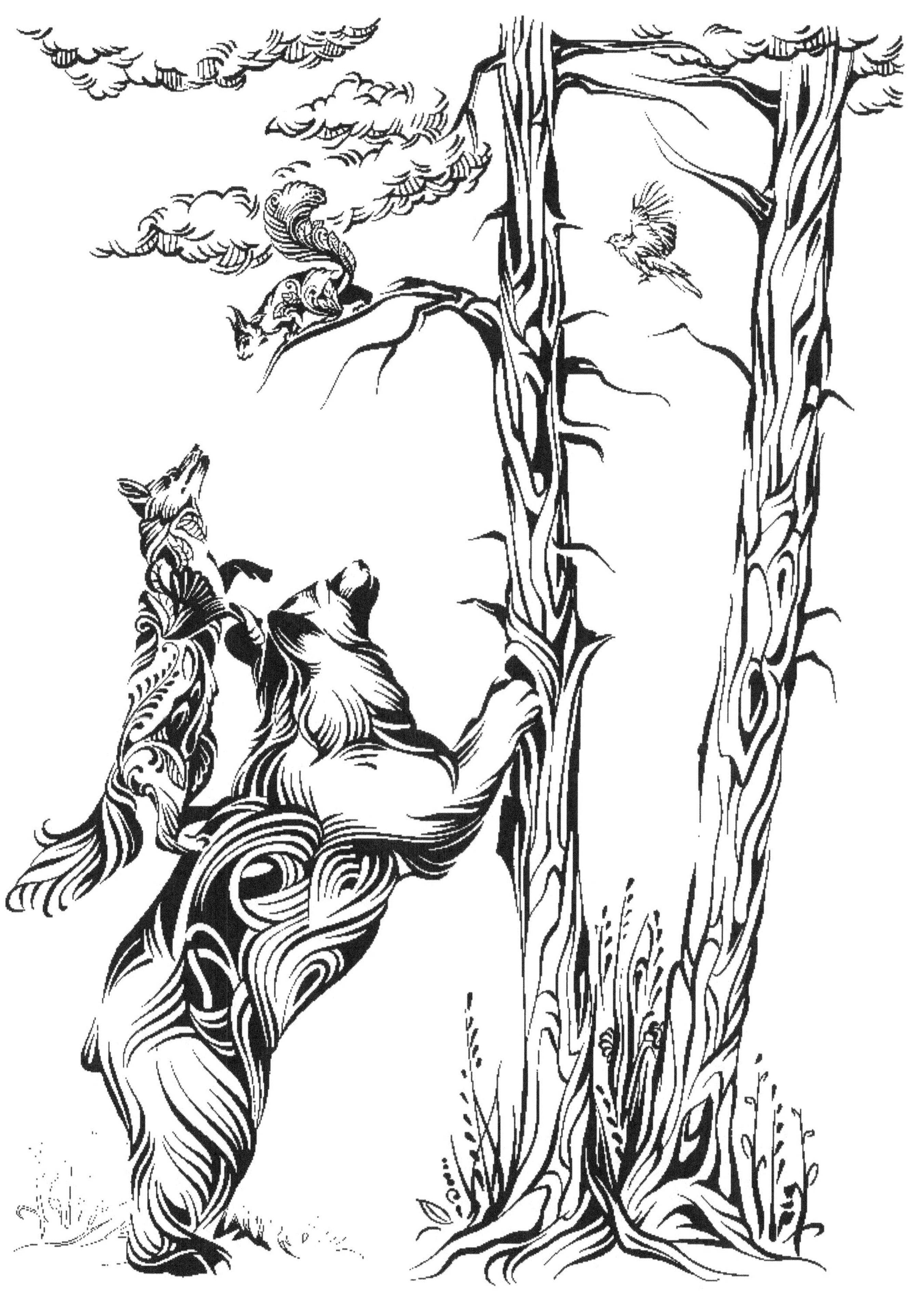

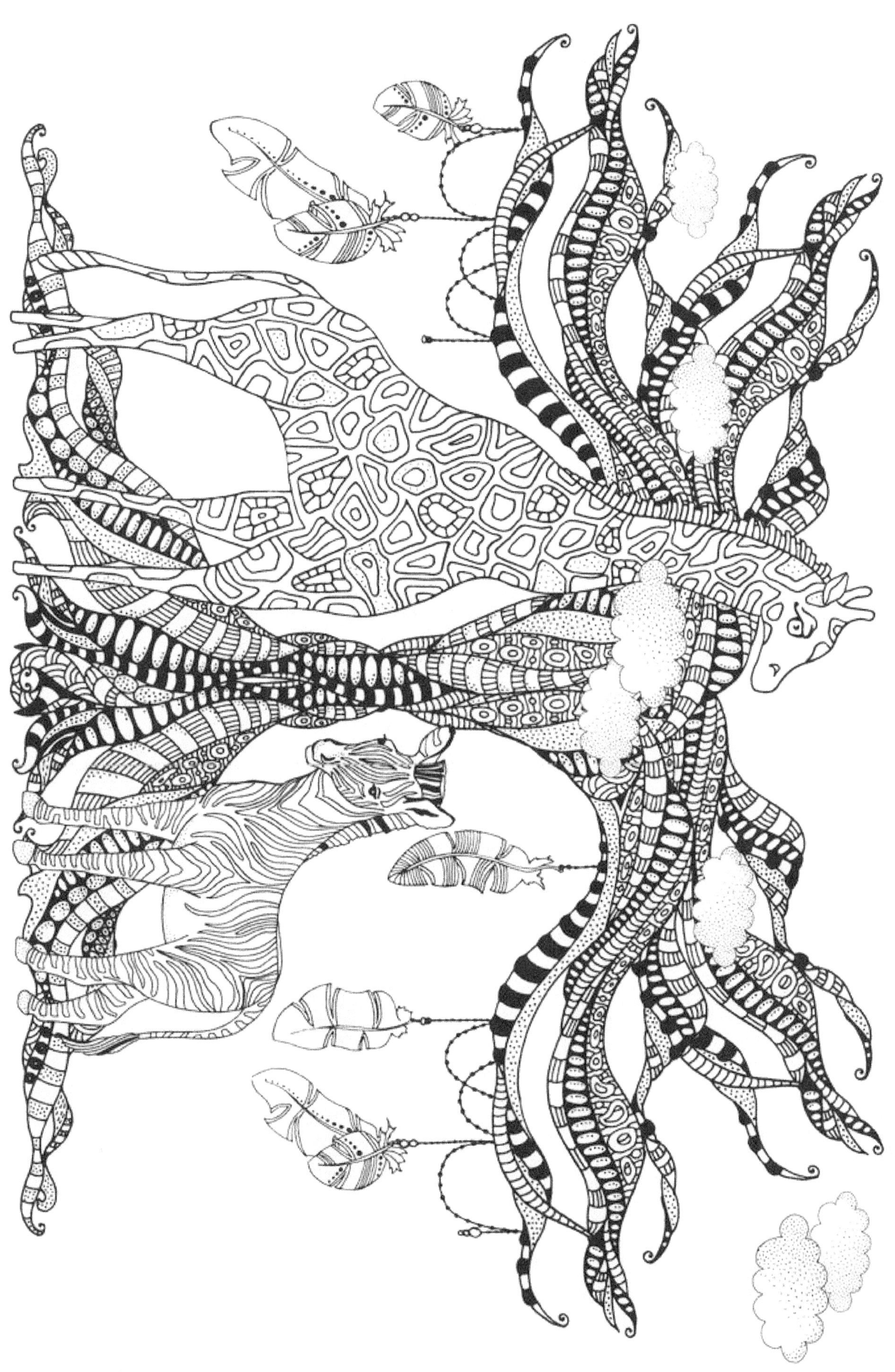

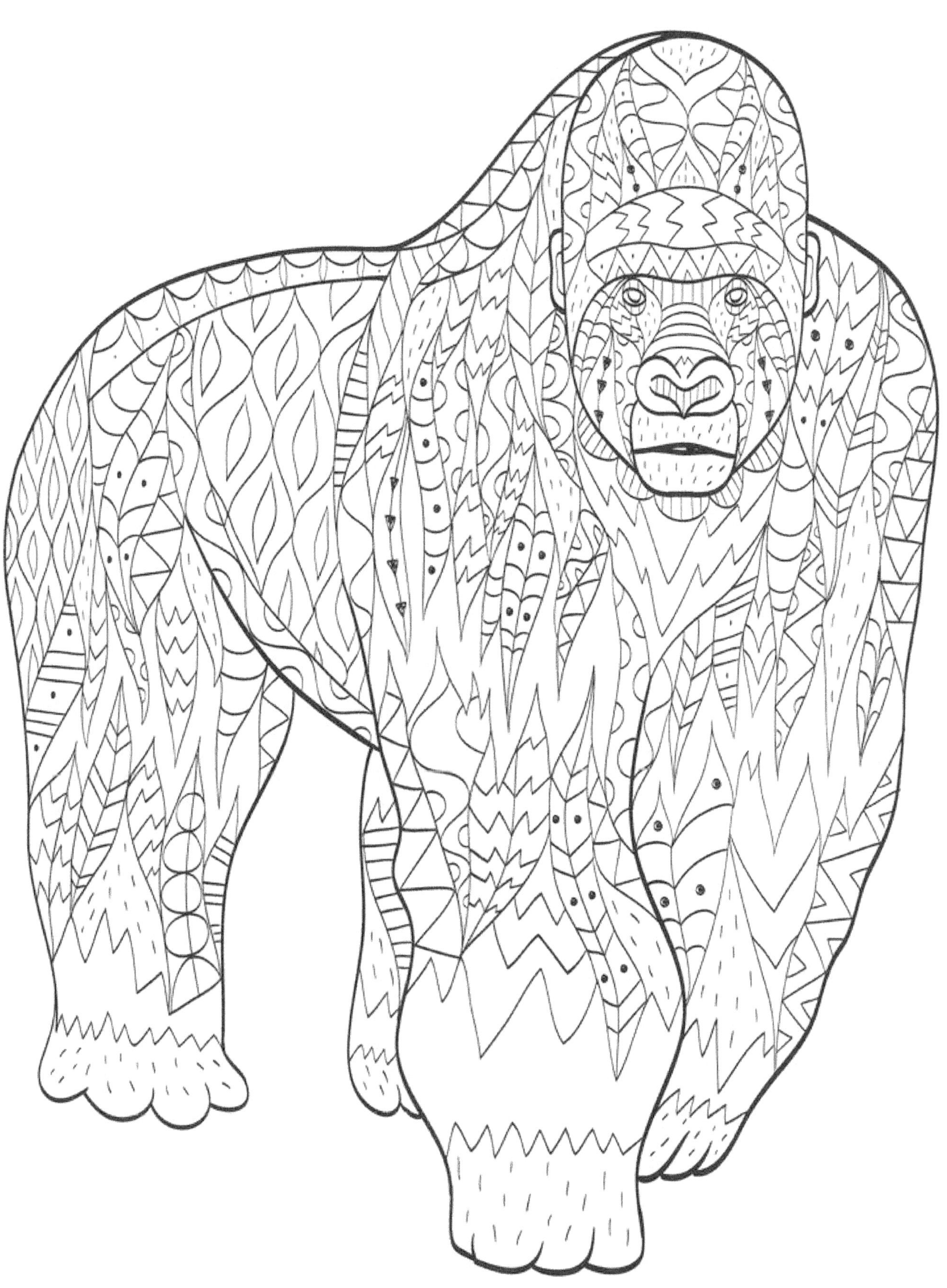

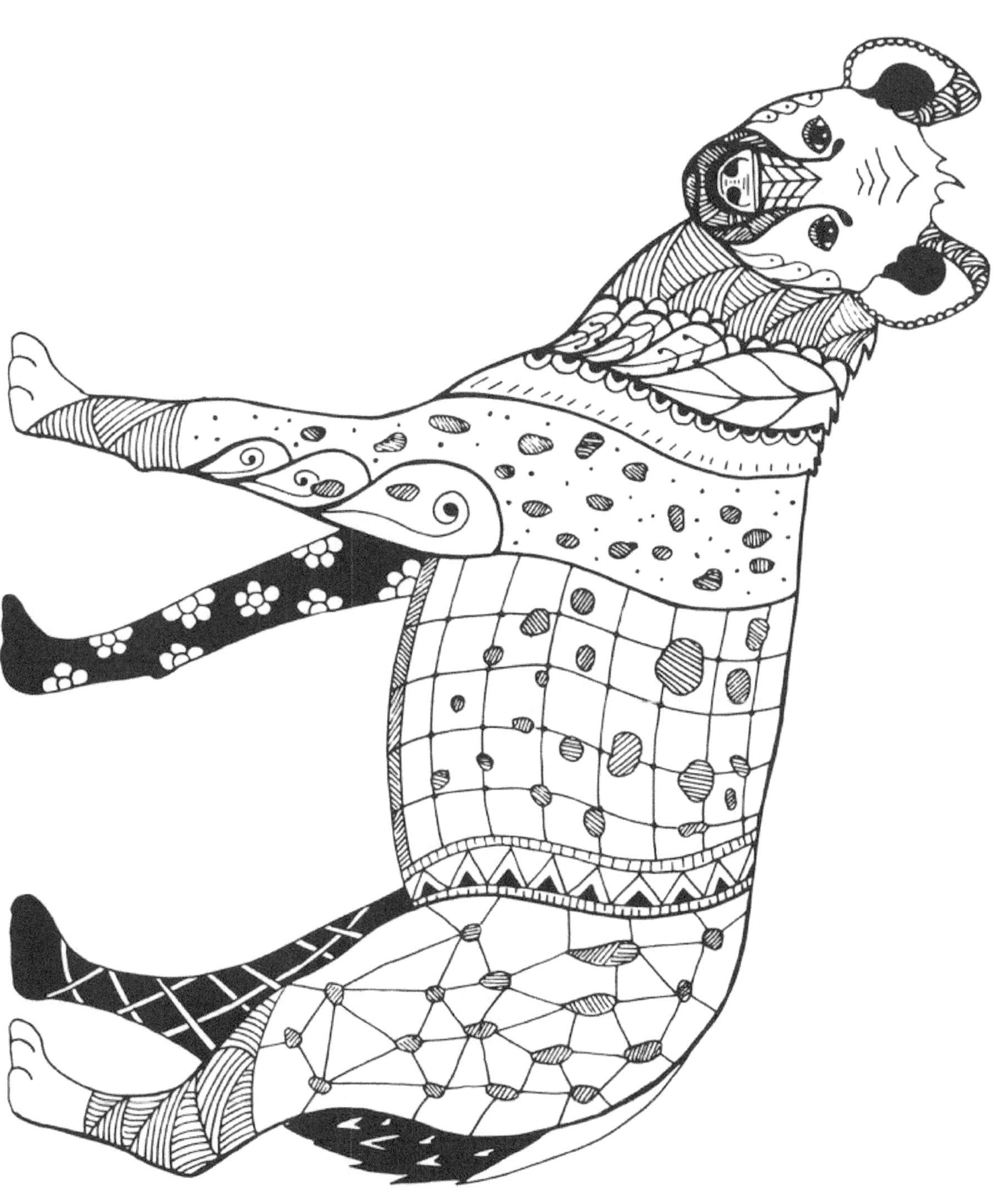

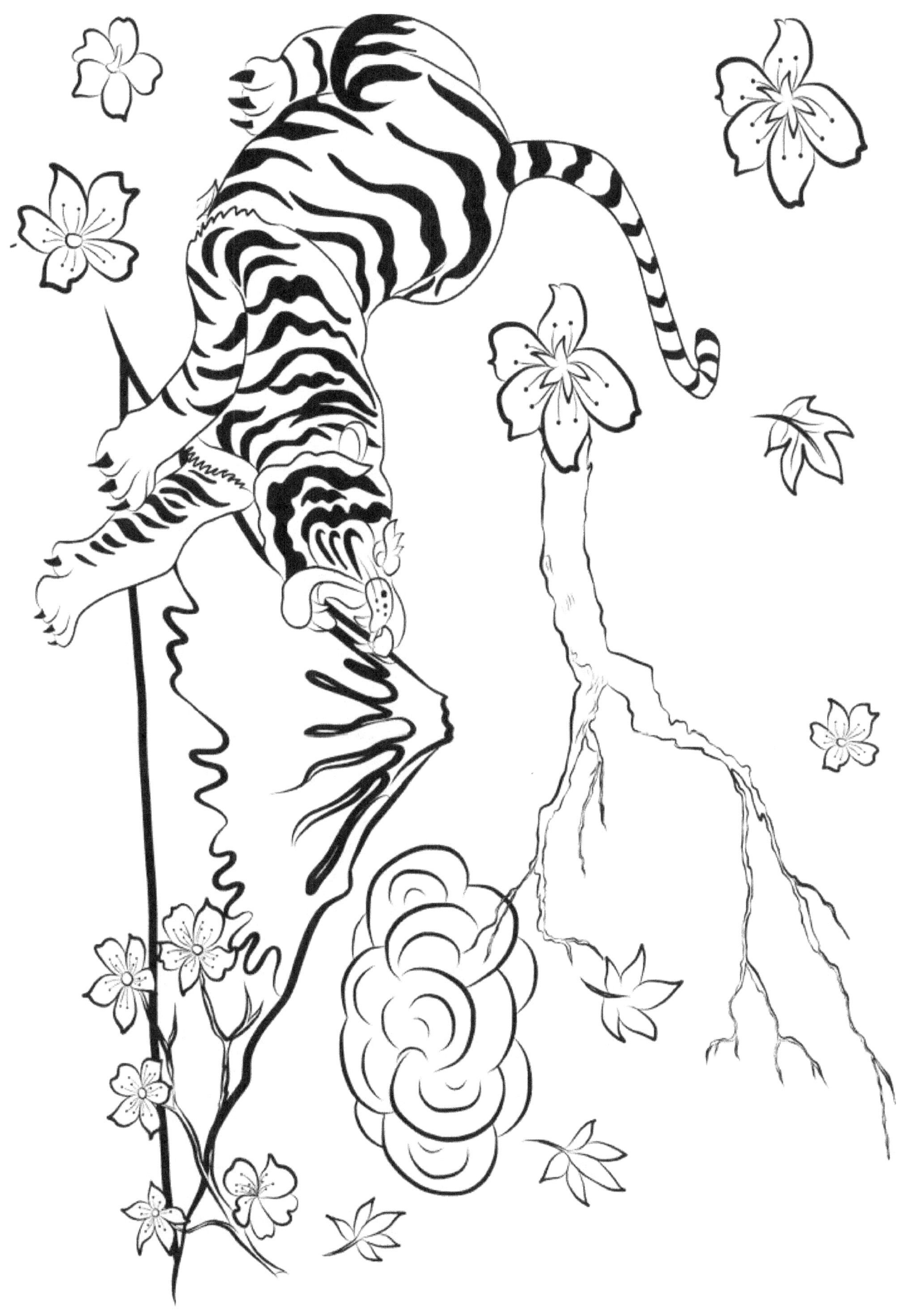

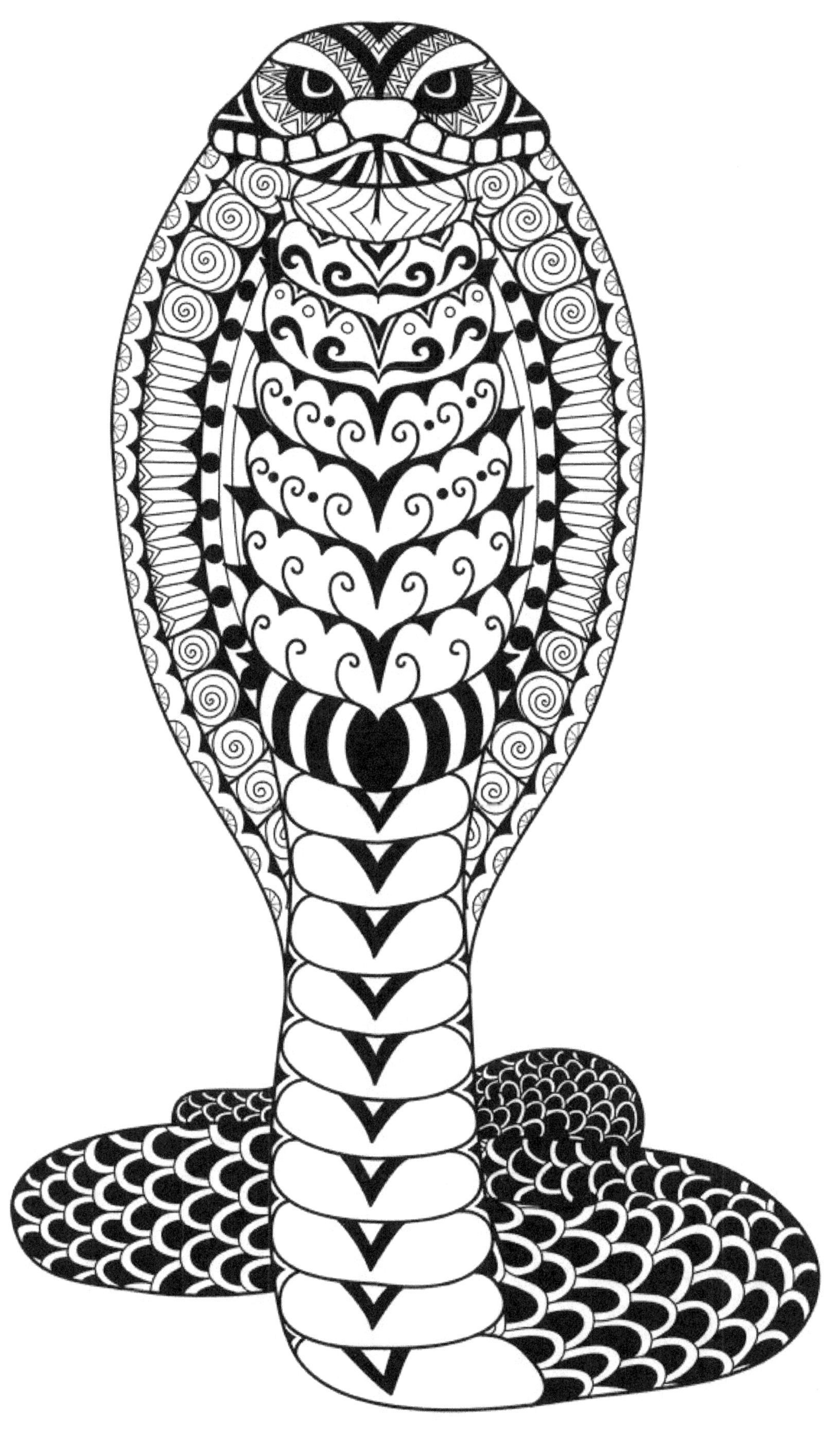

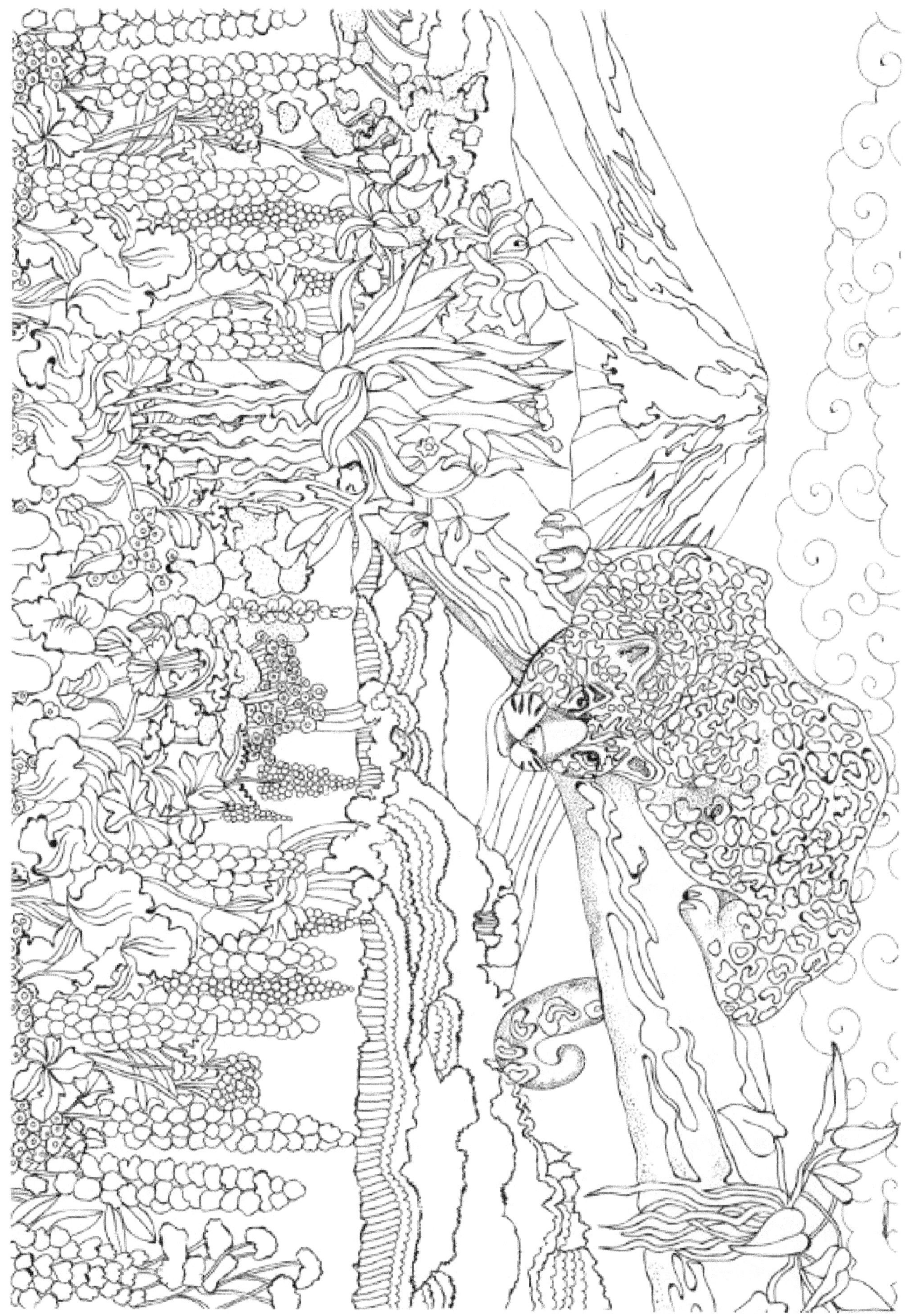

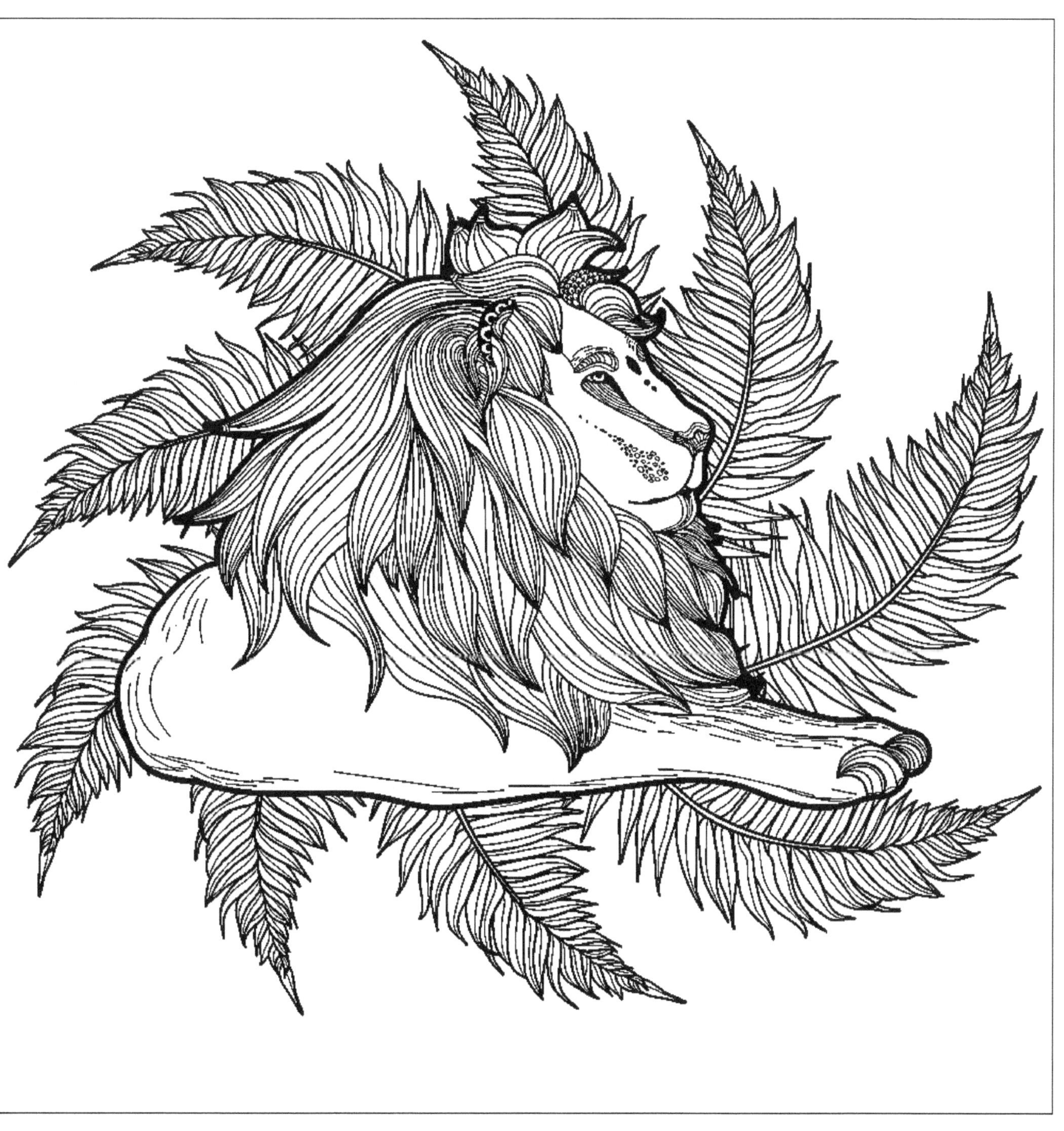

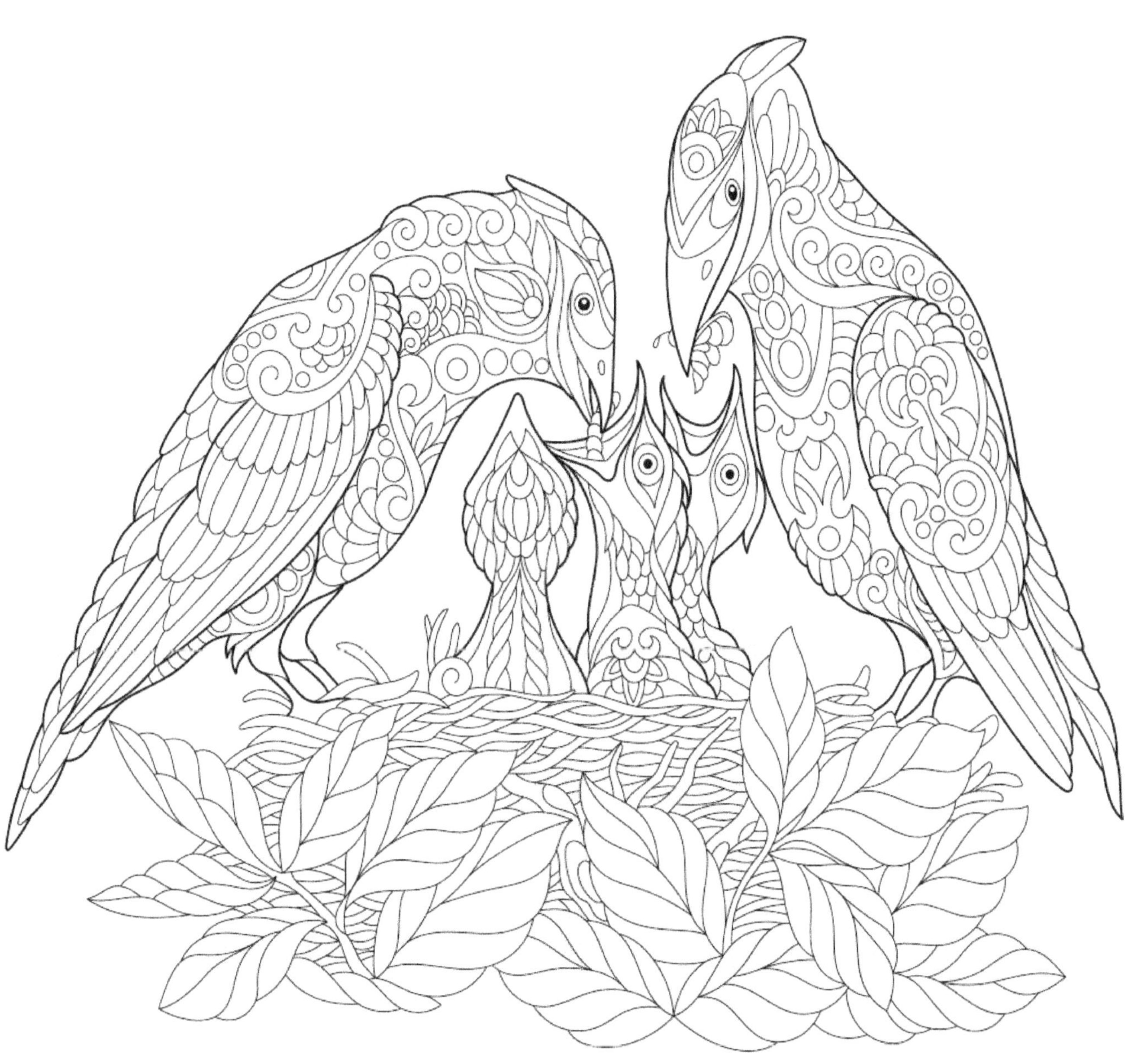

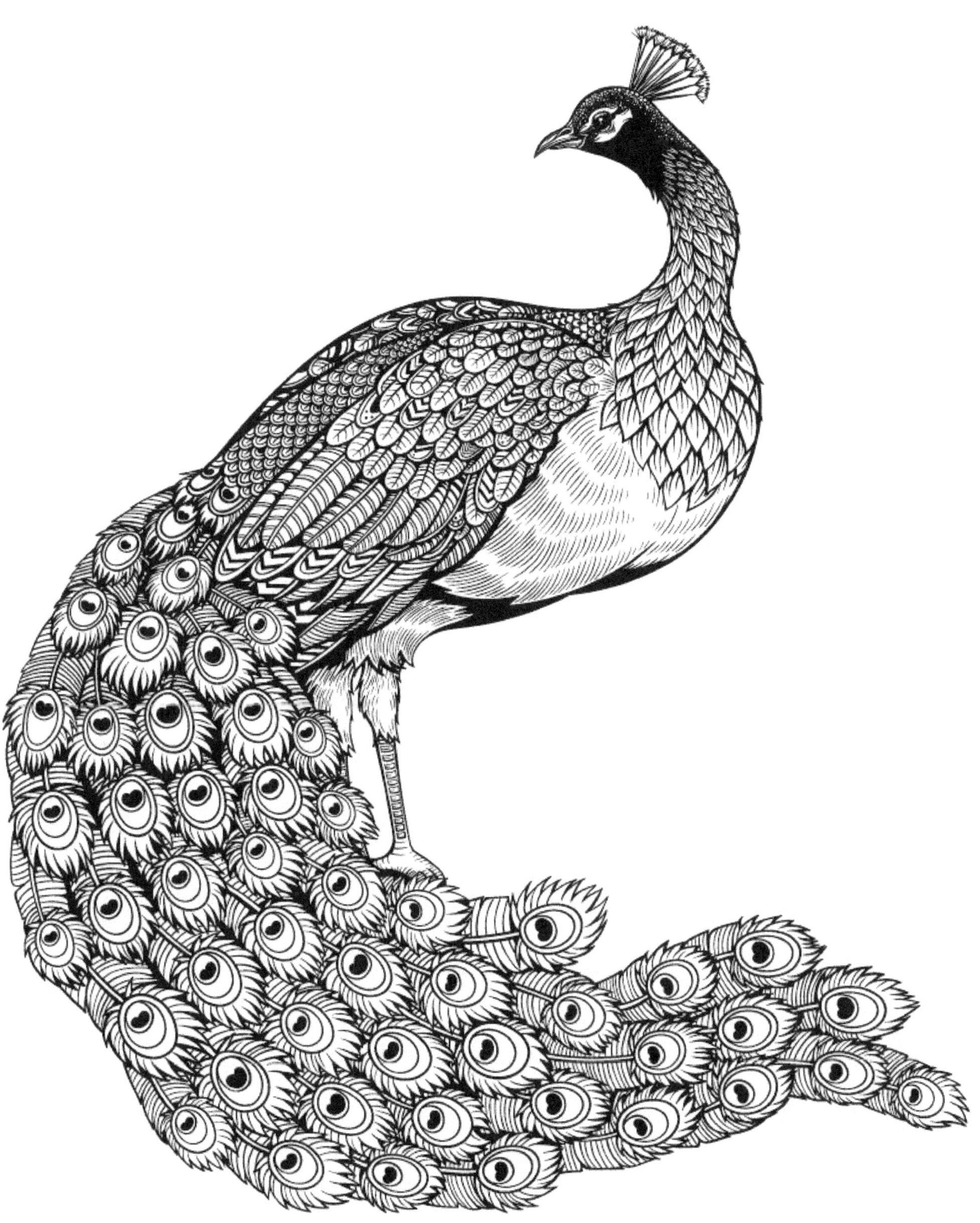

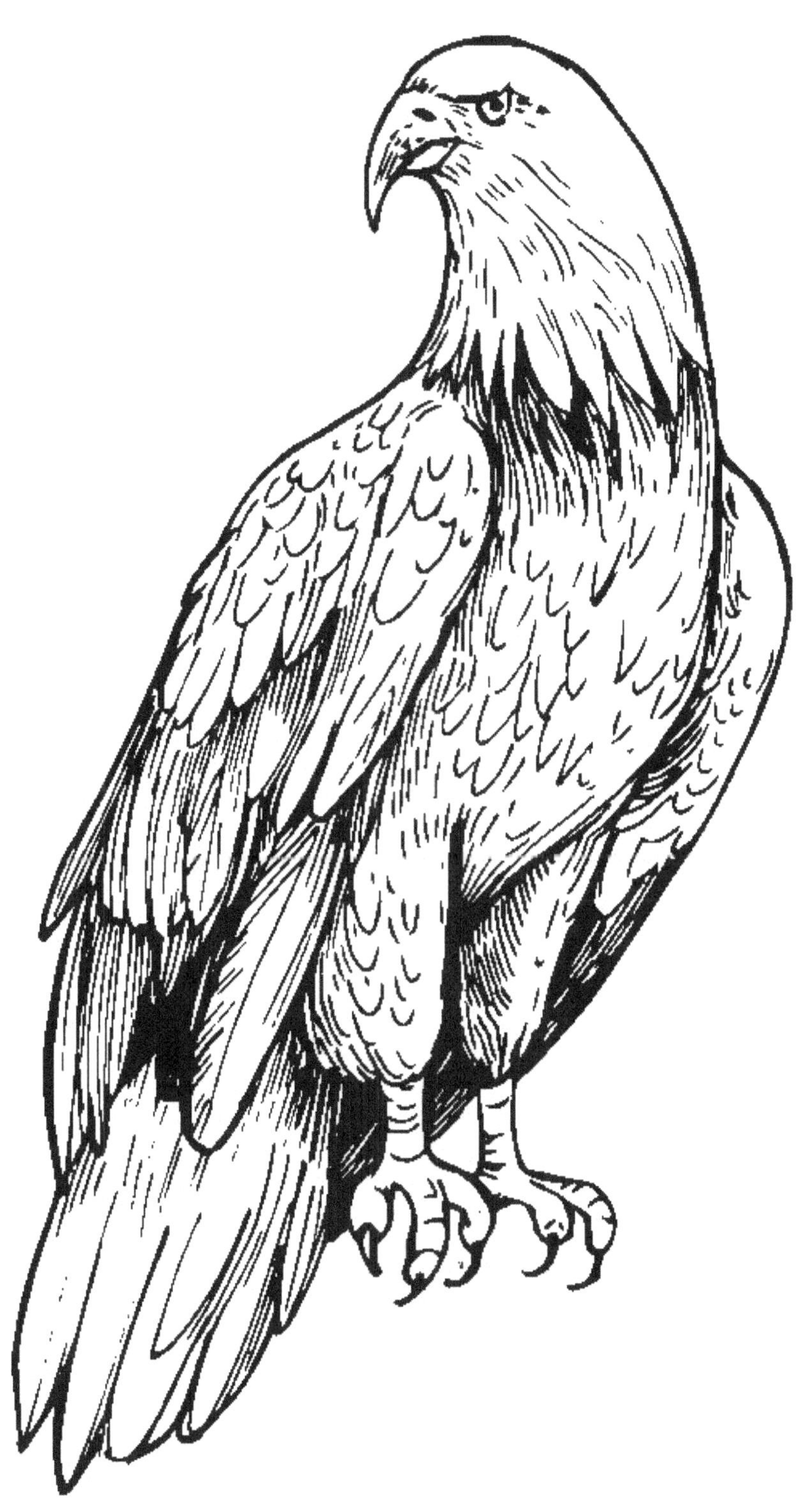

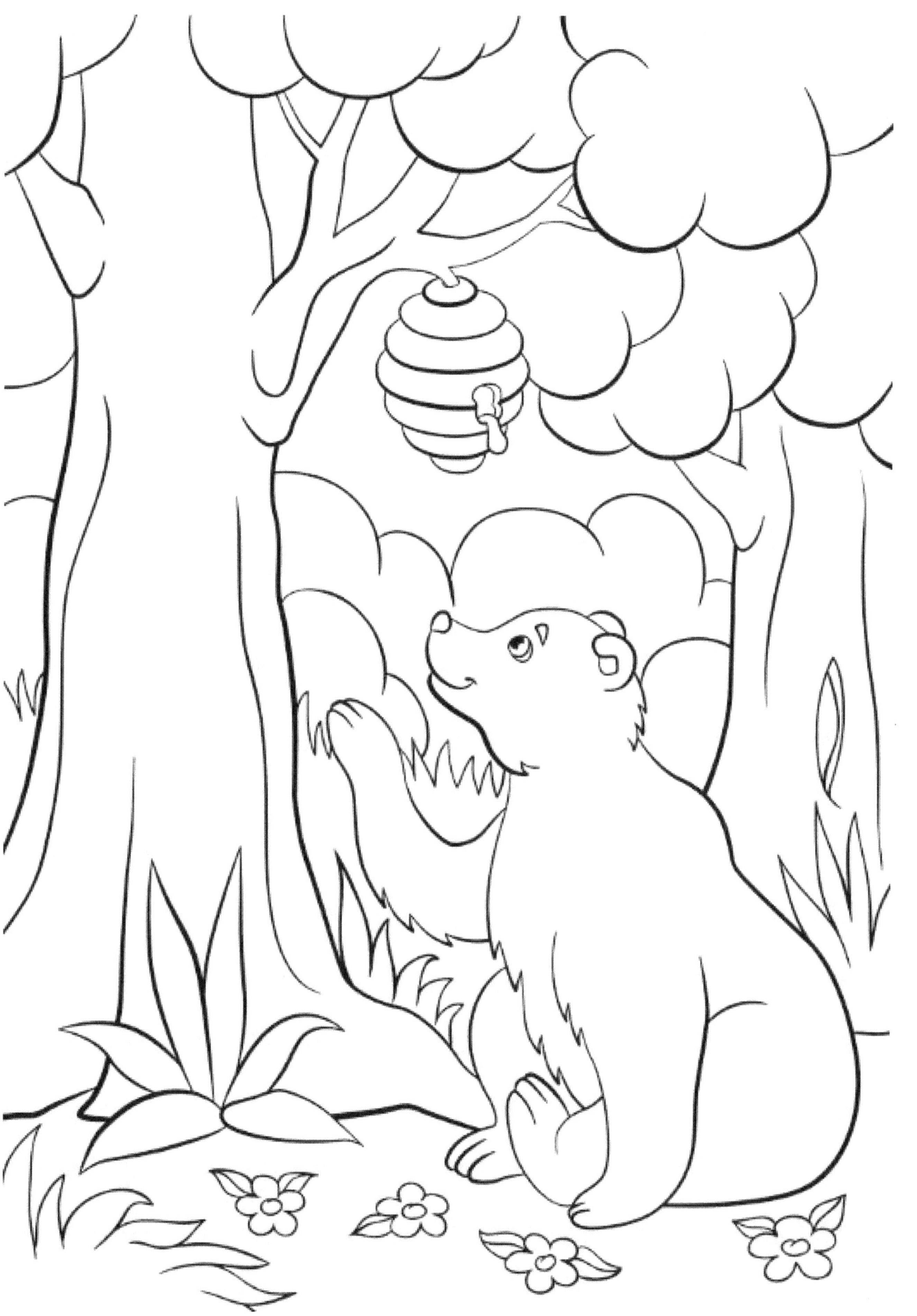

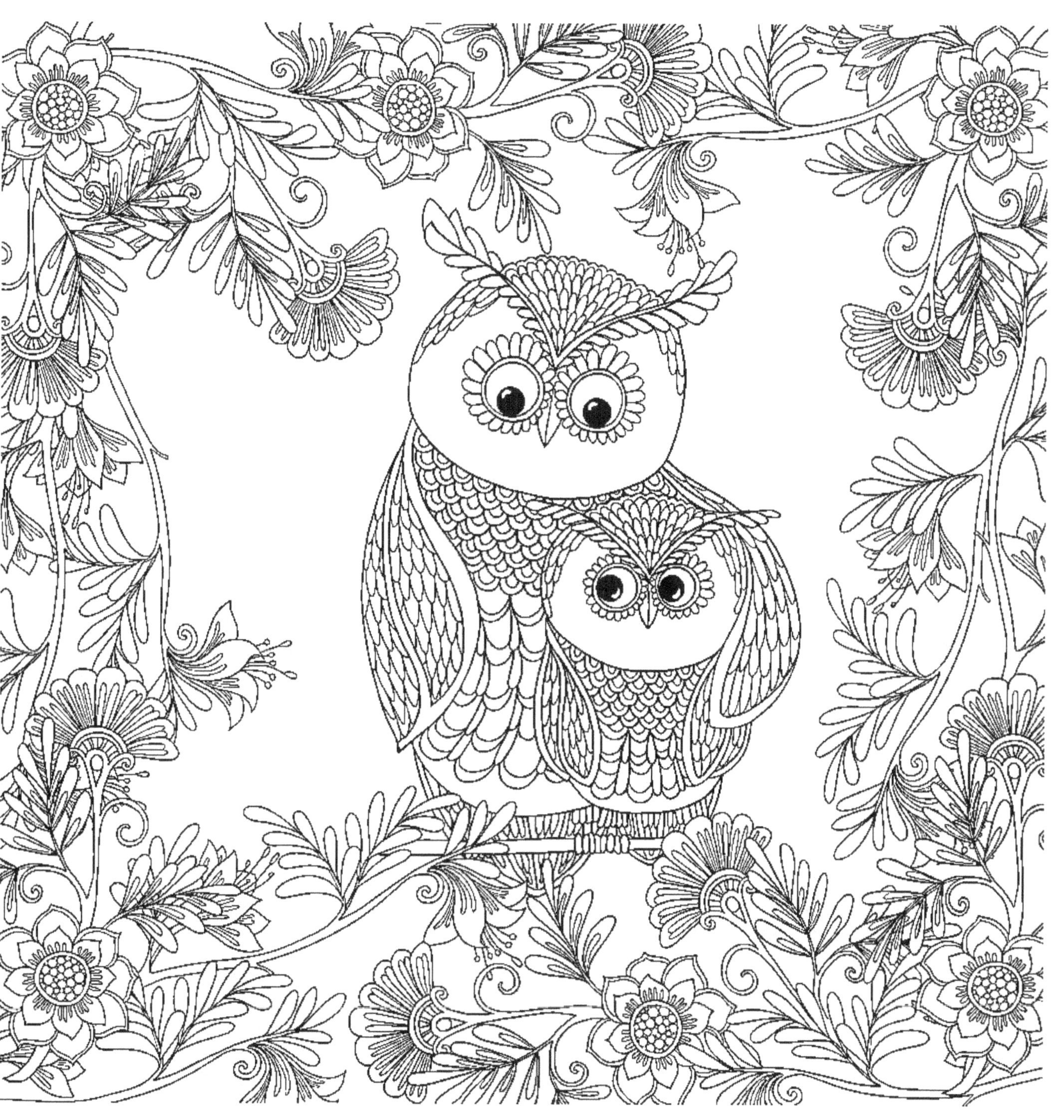

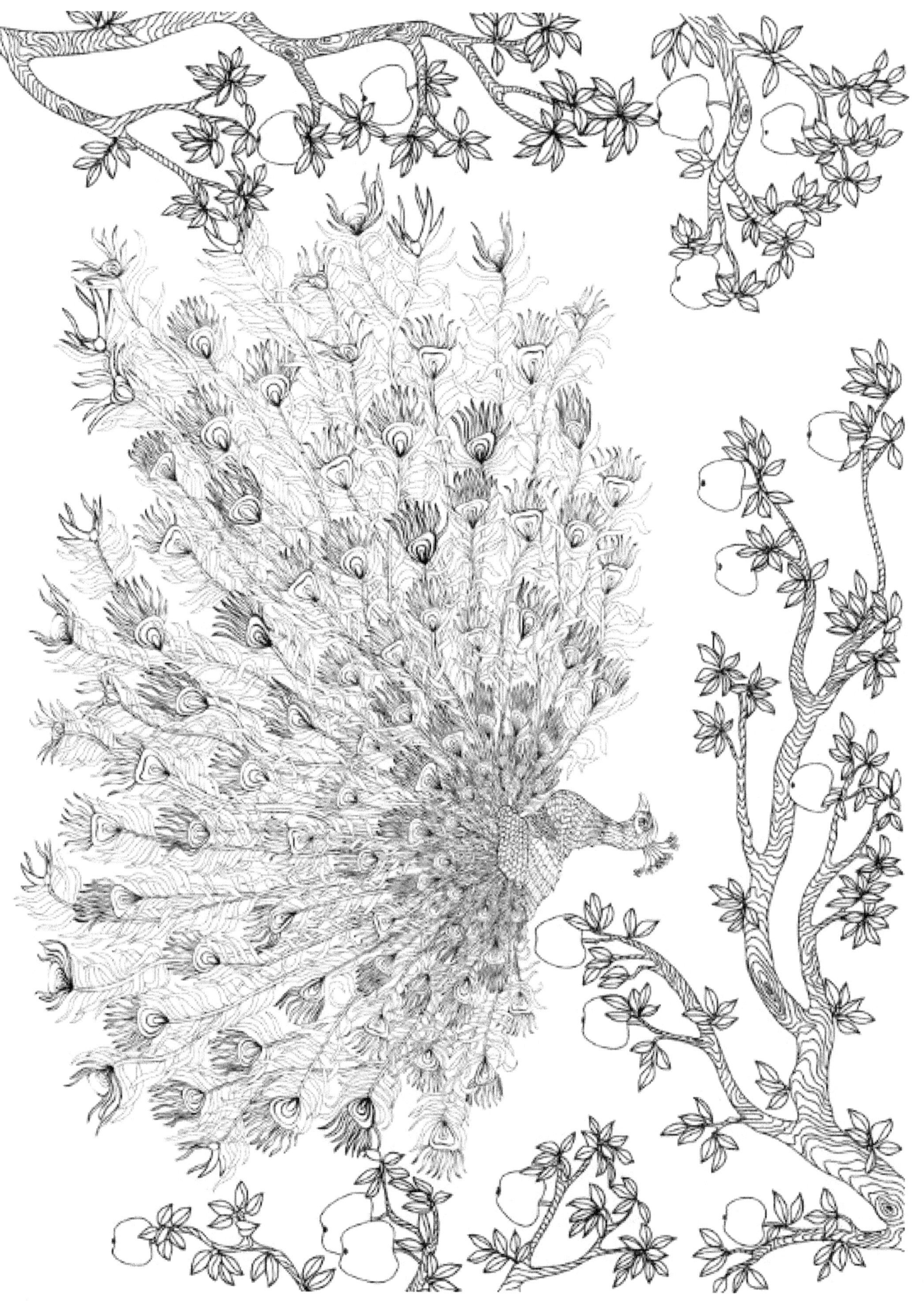